JAMAICA

ROBIN GAULDIE

> ★★★ Highly recommended
> ★★ Recommended
> ★ See if you can

This edition first published in 2001
by New Holland Publishers (UK) Ltd
London • Cape Town • Sydney • Auckland
First edition published in 1998
10 9 8 7 6 5 4 3 2 1

Garfield House, 86 Edgware Road
London W2 2EA
United Kingdom

80 McKenzie Street
Cape Town 8001
South Africa

14 Aquatic Drive
Frenchs Forest, NSW 2086
Australia

218 Lake Road
Northcote, Auckland
New Zealand

Distributed in the USA by
The Globe Pequot Press
Connecticut

Copyright © 2001 in text: Robin Gauldie
Copyright © 2001 in maps: Globetrotter Travel Maps
Copyright © 2001 in photographs:
Individual photographers as credited
Copyright © 1998, 2001 New Holland Publishers
(UK) Ltd

All rights reserved. No part of this publication
may be reproduced, stored in a retrieval system
or transmitted, in any form or by any means,
electronic, mechanical, photocopying, recording
or otherwise, without the prior written permission
of the publishers and copyright holders.

ISBN 185974 825 2

Commissioning Editor: Tim Jollands
Manager Globetrotter Maps: John Loubser
Managing Editor: Thea Grobbelaar
Editors: Tarryn Berry, Sean Fraser
Design and DTP: Nicole Engeler, Éloïse Moss
Cartographers: Elaine Fick, Genené Hart
Picture Researchers: Colleen Abrahams, Rowena Curtis

Reproduction by Hirt & Carter (Pty) Ltd, Cape Town
Printed and bound in Hong Kong by Sing Cheong
Printing Co. Ltd

Although every effort has been made to ensure
accuracy of facts, telephone and fax numbers in this
book, the publishers will not be held responsible for
changes that occur at the time of going to press.

Photographic Credits:
John Burke, 35, 41; **Abbie Enock**, 34, 76, 80, 83; **Robin Gauldie**, 4, 21, 94, 97, 118; **Image Select**, 14, 22, 30, 36; **Life File/Sue Davies**, 112, 115, 117; **Life File/Sean Finnigan**, 66, 69; **Life File/Juliet Highet**, 73 (top), 92; **Life File/Emma Lee**, 12, 24; **Photobank/Jeanetta Baker**, 6, 79; **Photobank/Peter Baker**, cover, title page, 19, 25, 62, 81, 85, 90, 93; **Richard Sale**, 7, 9, 11, 13, 15, 16, 17, 18, 20, 23, 26, 27, 33, 37, 39, 40, 42, 43, 44, 45, 48, 50, 51, 52, 53, 55, 56, 57, 58, 59, 65, 67, 70, 72, 73 (bottom), 84, 86, 87, 95, 98, 99, 102, 105, 106, 108, 109, 110; **Travel Ink/Simon Reddy**, 29; **Laurence Wood**, 28, 116.

Cover: *A picturesque scene of Negril, currently Jamaica's fastest-growing resort area.*
Title page: *Extensive white-sand beaches fringe the Ocho Rios area, one of the most thriving resorts in the Caribbean.*

CONTENTS

1. Introducing Jamaica 5
The Land 6
History in Brief 11
Government and Economy 19
The People 21

2. Kingston and St Andrew 31
Downtown Kingston 33
New Kingston and Old Hope Road 35
Port Royal 38
St Andrew Parish 42
Blue Mountains 44

3. Portland and St Thomas 49
Port Antonio 50
West of Port Antonio 53
Moore Town 54
East Coast 55
Bath 56
St Thomas Coast 57

4. St Ann and St Mary 63
Ocho Rios Area 64
Port Maria 69
St Ann's Bay 70
Runaway Bay 71
Discovery Bay 73

5. St James, Trelawny and Hanover 77
Montego Bay 78
St James Parish 81
Falmouth 83
The Cockpit Country 84
Hanover Parish 85
Lucea 87

6. Westmoreland and St Elizabeth 91
Negril 92
Westmoreland Parish 95
St Elizabeth Parish 97

7. Manchester, Clarendon and St Catherine 103
Mandeville and Surrounds 104
South Coast 107
May Pen 107
Spanish Town 108
Portmore 110

8. The Cayman Islands 113
Grand Cayman 114
Cayman Brac 117
Little Cayman 119

Travel Tips 122
Index 127

1
Introducing Jamaica

You know beyond a doubt when you have arrived in Jamaica. The weather is warmer, the insistent pulse of reggae music is on the air, and the cooling breeze from the Caribbean brings a whiff of poinsettia flowers, coconut oil, rum punch and a hint of ganja – the distilled aroma of a Jamaican holiday.

Jamaica is a rapidly developing country. The capital, **Kingston**, is a city of more than a million people, with all the urban potential of a fast-growing capital. Dotted around the island's shores are dozens of holiday **resorts**. Offering everything from barefoot simplicity to up-market sophistication or round-the-clock entertainment, they attract hundreds of thousands of visitors annually from Europe, North and South America and even Japan.

However, there is little overlap between urban Kingston and tourist Jamaica, and there are other aspects of Jamaican life that most visitors usually only get to glimpse from an air-conditioned minibus. In little villages in the hilly interior, rural folk work on sugar and coffee plantations or continue to scratch a living outside the cash economy from tiny patches of land.

In the mysterious, impenetrable jungle valleys of the **Cockpit Country**, the proud **Maroon** people maintain customs and a unique dialect closer in many ways to their West African ancestors than to the forward-looking young professionals of Kingston. Amazingly, some stretches of Jamaica's coast have not yet felt the full impact of tourism and primitive fishing canoes hollowed from a single tree trunk still stand in place of jet skis.

Top Attractions

*** **Negril:** lively but laid back, with the best beach, restaurants and nightlife.
*** **Montego Bay:** busiest resort, with good beaches and great shopping.
*** **Port Antonio:** peace and quiet amid gorgeous scenery.
** **Blue Mountain Peak:** finest view in Jamaica.
** **Rio Grande:** river rafting through giant bamboo forests.
** **YS Falls:** walk to the top, then plunge into the pools.
** **Black River:** Cruise through virgin forest and meet a crocodile.

Opposite: *Colourful tour boats line the mouth of the Negril River.*

Fact File

Geography: 146 miles (239km) east–west, 51 miles (82km) north–south at widest, with total land area 4244 sq miles (11,000km²).
Highest point: Blue Mountain Peak, 7402ft (2256m).
Government: Constitutional monarchy, independent of the UK since 1962. The Queen is formal head of state, represented by a governor general, with political and legislative power exercised by an elected two-chamber parliament and prime minister.
Population: 2.5 million, almost all of mixed African-European descent with small numbers of Chinese (less than 1%) and Middle Eastern (less than 5%) descent.

THE LAND

Jamaica is the biggest island in the English-speaking Caribbean and the third largest in the entire Caribbean region. It lies approximately 500 miles (800km) south of Miami, and its nearest neighbours are Cuba, less than 80 miles (130km) to the north, Haiti, about the same distance to the east, and the tiny Cayman Islands to the west. Shaped like a long, irregular oval, Jamaica is some 150 miles (240km) from east to west and 50 miles (80km) from north to south.

It is, in many respects, the embodiment of the Caribbean dream island. If your taste in holidays embraces sandy beaches, warm waters in a dozen tones of blue and turquoise, and a steady flow of delicious tropical cocktails, Jamaica approaches perfection.

However, there is much more to Jamaica. Behind every beach resort, hillsides cloaked in shades of tropical green beckon you to explore further this fascinating island. When Christopher Columbus came to Jamaica in 1493 he discovered a land of well-watered virgin forests, named by its indigenous Arawak people **Xaymaca** – 'the land of wood and water'. That name is still very apt today, despite five centuries of settlement and the introduction of sugar cane and coffee plantations, bauxite mines, and modern towns and resort complexes. Landing on a Jamaican beach today, Columbus would probably be astounded by the tourist development, but he would still be able to recognise the woods, rivers and waterfalls of his Jamaica.

THE LAND

Mountains and Rivers

Inland, much of the country is ruggedly mountainous. Jamaica is in fact a relatively high island, with almost half land at an altitude of over 1000ft (300m). In the east, not far from Kingston, Jamaica's highest summit rises from the **Blue Mountain** range to a height of 7402ft (2256m), while the **John Crow Mountains** continue further to the east. In the western part of the island the thickly-wooded limestone hills of the **Cockpit Country**, with their curious karst rock formations – once dubbed 'The Land of Look Behind' – are still mostly trackless, to be explored only on foot.

Although it has many small streams, Jamaica has only a few proper rivers. The **Rio Grande**, rising in the Portland mountains, and the **Great River**, forming the boundary between St James and Hanover, are the largest – though neither more than 66ft (20m) at its widest. There are no natural or manmade lakes.

Seas and Shores

Kingston lies on the south coast, about 40 miles (64km) from the east end of the island and on a natural harbour. The capital is home to almost one in three Jamaicans, and is Jamaica's only big city. But it is the north coast which

Above: *San San Bay's beautiful waters have made it an exclusive resort area.*
Opposite: *The Great River is one of the largest watercourses in Jamaica.*

GREEN FLASH

No visitor who has been privileged to glimpse it will soon forget the green flash. This rare phenomenon of the Caribbean sky occurs just as the last sliver of sun sets below the horizon. If the sky is absolutely clear of cloud, dust and pollutants – an increasingly rare occurrence – light refraction through the atmosphere can cause a vivid emerald flash which can last for two seconds.

> **CLIMATE**
>
> At 18°N of the Equator, Jamaica has a **hot** and **humid** climate year round with almost no regional variation around the coast, though steady breezes on the **north coast** – the **Doctor Breeze** – make it more pleasant than **Kingston**, which swelters in a sheltered bowl of mountains with little relief from the heat. On the coast, temperatures average 28°C (82°F), with a maximum of 32°C (90°F) and a minimum of 27°C (80°F). On higher ground, around **Mandeville**, temperatures average around 6°C (11°F) less than on the coast. On the heights of the **Blue Mountains**, temperatures average 9°C (16°F) less than at sea level. July to October is hurricane season, and although hurricanes are far from an annual event, tropical storms and frequent downpours make the island somewhat less attractive to visitors during these months.

has traditionally seen the lion's share of Jamaica's tourism development. **Montego Bay** boasts Jamaica's second international airport and both 'Mo Bay' (Montego Bay) and **Ocho Rios**, midway along the north coast, are popular ports of call with US-based cruise ships. Beach resorts and villa complexes occupy almost every stretch of sandy beach between the two. **Port Antonio**, further east on the north coast, is another centre for more upmarket tourism.

Jamaica's south coast sees far fewer tourists by comparison. An exception is **Negril**, on the extreme southwest corner of the island, which has rocketed from sleepy fishing village to full-scale international resort status in less than two decades, and is currently Jamaica's fastest-growing resort area.

Climate

While Jamaica's coast basks in tropical sunshine for much of the year, with little variation in temperature, settlements in the hilly hinterland enjoy cooler temperatures, especially at night.

By the sea, the temperature averages 28°C (82°F) year-round, rising as high as the low 30s at midday and falling into the mid-20s at night. Sunscreen is an essential; air-conditioning is usually not. In the highlands around Mandeville, temperatures average around 21°C (70°F) year-round, while in the heights of the Blue Mountains, days – and especially nights – are much cooler than on the coast. Annual rainfall averages 78 inches (1980mm). It can rain heavily at any time of year, but the heaviest rainfall is between May and November. Naturally, this is the least popular time to visit the island, though many visitors from the UK and continental Europe come to Jamaica during these hot and humid months, to take advantage of the low off-season hotel prices. Most North American visitors, however, tend to come to Jamaica only during the winter months.

JAMAICA	J	F	M	A	M	J	J	A	S	O	N	D
AVERAGE TEMP. °C	30	30	30	32	32	33	33	33	33	32	32	32
AVERAGE TEMP. °F	86	86	86	90	90	92	92	92	92	90	90	90
HOURS OF SUN DAILY	10	10	10	9	9	6	6	6	6	4	4	9
RAINFALL mm	25	25	25	75	100	75	50	100	150	175	150	25
RAINFALL in.	1	1	1	3	4	3	2	4	6	7	6	1
DAYS OF RAINFALL	1	1	1	6	7	6	5	10	12	14	12	1

THE LAND

The south coast receives much less rain than the north, and the northeast – in the shadow of the Blue Mountains – is the wettest part of the island.

Like all Caribbean islands, Jamaica is occasionally hit badly by hurricanes – most recently by Hurricane Gilbert in 1988 – though modern hurricane forecasting and warning systems help minimise damage to property and loss of life. Hurricanes and smaller tropical storms are most likely to occur in July and August. The Jamaican proverb runs: 'June, too soon; July, stand by; August, you must; September, remember; October, all over.'

Wildlife

Jamaica shares many plants and animals with other Caribbean islands and with the Americas, and there are also many species endemic to the islands. Unfortunately, some Jamaican bird and reptile populations have been reduced because of loss of habitat and predation by pests, which prey on eggs and fledglings. Nevertheless, Jamaica still has more than 250 **bird species**, 26 of which are indigenous. They range in size from the tiny **bee hummingbird** – the smallest of four species of hummingbird found in Jamaica – to giants like the **frigate bird**, an unmistakable predator with its long, hooked bill, forked tail, pointed wings and black plumage. Seen everywhere is the **'John Crow'**, a buzzard which circles high above the streets, hillsides and beaches alike. Another scavenger, the bright-eyed, glossy-black **Antillean grackle**, will hop onto your table to steal scraps.

Reptiles indigenous to the island include the **Jamaican iguana** and the rare **American crocodile**, while **mammals** include the rabbit-like **coney** – a species of agouti – and the harmless vegetarian **manatee** sometimes spotted swimming in south coast bays and rivers.

> **HURRICANES**
>
> Appropriately for such a savage people, the cannibal **Caribs** had a savage god – **Huracan**, the mighty wind that scourges the Caribbean. Hurricane season is August–October. These giant circular wind systems gusting up to 185mph (300kph) are born when northeast and southeast trade winds meet in mid-Atlantic, and are swept westward by the earth's rotation. **Hurricane Gilbert** hit Jamaica on 12 September 1988, devastating crops and destroying roads, family homes, businesses and even power supplies. Jamaicans have more or less come to accept such disasters as facts of life.

Below: *Rare crocodiles are found at the Great Morass in St Elizabeth Parish.*

Plant Life

Like its wildlife, Jamaica's plantlife is a mixture of native and exotic. The **royal palm**, native to the island, is far outnumbered by the coconut variety, an import from the East Indies. Other native plants include the **pineapple**, **guava**, **soursop**, **pimento**, and the **lignum vitae** tree. More than 500 kinds of **fern** flourish in the steamy climate, as do **orchids** – more than 200 species – and **bromeliads**.

Sugar Cane

Sugar cane is still one of the island's biggest crops but it brings in less foreign currency than newer industries. While processing of the cane is now mechanised, much of the field work is done by hand and wages remain low.

Historical Calendar

7th century AD Arawak people from South America settle in the island they call Xaymaca, 'the land of wood and water'.

15th century AD Also from South America, fierce Carib people arrive to prey on the less aggressive Arawaks.

1493 Christopher Columbus makes landfall at St Ann's Bay.

1503–4 On his fourth voyage of discovery, Columbus spends a year at St Ann's Bay repairing his ships.

1510 First Spanish colony, Sevilla la Nueva, established. Soon the native Arawaks are virtually wiped out.

1517 Spaniards introduce the first African slaves.

1534 New Spanish base established at Santiago de la Vega (Spanish Town).

1655 British invasion force ousts Spaniards. Slaves left by the departing Spaniards escape into the uninhabited mountains, where they form the first Maroon settlements.

1658 Spaniards try to recover the island but are defeated at Battle of Rio Nuevo.

1660s Port Royal becomes a notorious haven for a buccaneer fleet under the British flag which harries Spanish fleets and colonies.

1670 Spain formally cedes Jamaica to Britain.

1690 First of several island-wide slave uprisings, led by Cudjoe. British troops and militia brutally crush the rebels and their Maroon allies in the first Maroon War.

1692 Earthquake destroys Port Royal.

1694 French fleet raids Jamaica but is beaten at Carlisle Bay.

1739 Maroon treaty gives the Maroons land and self government but obliges them to hunt out and return runaway slaves.

1760 Coromantee slave rebellion.

1795 Second Maroon War.

1807 Britain ends slave trade.

1831 Sam Sharpe's rebellion is brutally quelled.

1834 Britain abolishes slavery.

1865 Paul Bogle's rebellion is crushed and hundreds of rebels are executed.

1872 Kingston becomes seat of colonial government.

1907 More than 800 Jamaicans die in the great Kingston earthquake.

1938 Economic depression triggers riots and protests. The formation of People's National Party (PNP) by Norman Manley and first trade union organisation by Alexander Bustamante.

1944 Britain grants full self government to Jamaica.

1962 Jamaica becomes independent country within the British commonwealth. Sir Alexander Bustamante becomes first prime minister.

1972 PNP led by Michael Manley wins its first election.

1978 Bob Marley hosts concert to urge end to political violence.

1980 JLP (Jamaican Labour Party) led by Seaga wins election after a wave of pre-election violence in which several hundred people are killed.

1988 On 12 September, Hurricane Gilbert does great damage to homes, businesses and agriculture.

1989 The PNP returns to power on new moderate left platform.

1992 Michael Manley retires as PNP leader and prime minister of Jamaica.

1993 Manley's successor P.J. Patterson re-elected as prime minister.

1994 Air Jamaica privatised.

1996 Launch of Air Jamaica Express, Air Jamaica's intra-island airline.

1999 Tax on accommodation replaced by 15% general consumption tax.

1999 Two days of island-wide rioting in protest against fuel tax increases.

HISTORY IN BRIEF

In a region of microstates where the population is more often measured in tens of thousands than in millions, Jamaica's size, energy, and a long line of bold and outspoken leaders from every shade of the political and cultural spectrum have made it a pace-setter for many of its Caribbean neighbours.

Arawaks and Caribs

The earliest people to settle Jamaica were wiped out – along with their culture and language – by European settlers within two centuries of the arrival of the Spaniards, so we know little of them beyond what archaeological discoveries and the writings of the first Spanish navigators can tell us.

The placid **Arawaks**, who originated in what is now Venezuela, island-hopped through the Caribbean in their seagoing canoes over several centuries and seem to have arrived in Jamaica around 650AD. Living on the sea and on abundant native fruit and vegetables, they settled around the coast but ignored the mountainous, impenetrable jungles of the interior. The Arawak idyll lasted for some 750 years until it was brutally interrupted by the warlike **Caribs**. Of similar Amerindian origin, the Caribs arrived in fleets of canoes to prey on Arawak villages, looting, enslaving and, on occasion, eating their less aggressive cousins. A similar pattern prevailed throughout much of what is now known as the Caribbean, named by the European invaders after these early aggressors. Fierce though the Caribs were, however, there was much worse in store for the native peoples. By the latter half of the 17th century, both the Arawaks and Caribs had disappeared, victims of slavery, disease and deliberate genocide.

The Spanish Main

Christopher Columbus made landfall off St Ann's in 1493, ushering in more than three centuries of colonisation, war, piracy and slavery.

ARAWAKS

Jamaica's earliest settlers were the seafaring Arawaks, a native Amerindian people who journeyed in their huge dug-out canoes from the Caribbean coast of what is now **Venezuela**. There are traces of their settlements on almost all the Caribbean islands. Archaeological studies show that they lived all around the Jamaican coast, and numbered some 100,000 when Columbus arrived in Jamaica. They seem to have been a peaceful people, growing cassava, sweet potato and other vegetables to complement the seafood they caught, and dividing the island equably into provinces, each ruled by a chief called a **cacique**.

Left: *An exhibit from the Arawak Museum near Spanish Town.*

CARIBS

The fierce seafarers who gave the Caribbean its name originated, like the Arawak, in Central America, and fared through the Caribbean in giant canoes. But instead of settling peacefully, the Caribs ravaged the Arawaks, enslaving women and children and killing and eating the men. By Columbus' time, they had conquered the **Lesser Antilles** and were raiding Jamaica. Their ferocity failed to save them from the lethal impact of colonisation.

Despite all the evidence to the contrary, Columbus remained convinced that Jamaica and its neighbours lay close to the coast of China – the legendary Cathay – and its fabulous riches. Following in his wake, however, came a second wave of **Spanish** *conquistadors*, whose discoveries of Aztec and Inca gold in Mexico and Peru quickly put Jamaica in the shade. While the conquest of South America and its riches suddenly started to attract soldiers and settlers by the thousand, Jamaica became a backwater, valued only for the safe anchorages, fresh water and supplies it afforded Spanish vessels en route to more important Spanish colonies in the Americas. For approximately a century and a half, the Caribbean was known to Europe simply as the **Spanish Main**. Pirates and privateers – some of them under the flag of England, France or the Dutch Republic, others flying the Jolly Roger – regularly attacked Spain's treasure galleons, but Spain remained supreme until the 1660s.

Below: *Columbus' landfall eventually led to the full mapping of Jamaica.*

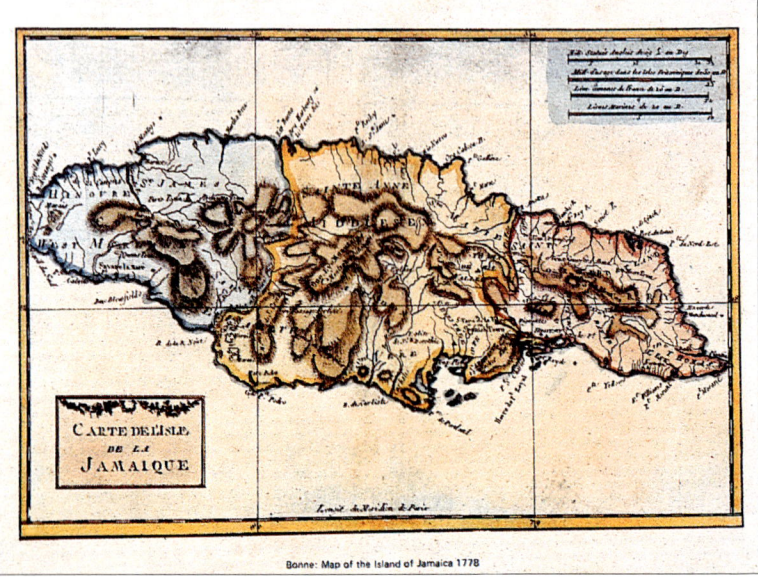

Bonne: Map of the Island of Jamaica 1778

The British Arrive

By the second half of the 17th century, Spain had been weakened by almost a century of wars with its European neighbours, and France, Britain and the Netherlands were all eyeing its lucrative Caribbean possessions.

In 1655, using the excuse of war with Spain in Europe, a **British** fleet sailed into what is now Kingston Harbour. With the British guns threatening their capital of Santiago de la Vega (today's **Spanish Town**) the Spanish garrison sailed off to the much stronger Spanish island colony of Cuba, leaving behind slaves whom they had freed and provided with weapons in the hope that they would fight a bush war against the British. Refusing to fight for their former masters, however, the freed slaves fled deep into the interior, where they set up little kingdoms. These **Maroons** (from the Spanish *cimarron*, meaning 'wild') were eventually to become a major problem for the British authorities, providing refuge for escaped slaves.

Some three years later, the Spanish troops returned and tried to drive the British out but were trounced at **Rio Nuevo**. Britain then set out to make life extremely uncomfortable for the Spanish colonies, raiding settlements and attacking supply fleets. Britain was not yet a world-class naval power, and throughout the 1660s the British government allowed privateers – pirates in all but name – to attack the Spaniards in the name of the Crown. In 1670 Spain formally surrendered Jamaica to England by signing the **Treaty of Madrid** and, despite an attempt by a **French** fleet under Admiral Jean du Casse to invade the island in 1694, Jamaica was to remain firmly in British hands for almost three centuries.

Buccaneers and Privateers

At first, British control of Jamaica was slack. Port Royal, the first British capital, which stood on the long spit of land sheltering Kingston Harbour quickly became a nest of pirates and was known as 'the wickedest city in the world'.

> **BUCCANEERS**
>
> The first buccaneers were a motley crew of **castaways** and **runaways** who lived by hunting wild boar and cattle, and curing meat – called *boucan* – to trade with passing ships for tools, powder and shot. They became known as *boucaniers* and when they formed an alliance, the **Brethren of the Coast**, to prey on Spanish shipping, the name became synonymous with piracy.
>
> France and England hired them with 'letters of marque and reprisal' to attack enemy shipping. In the **Dutch War** of 1665 they saved Jamaica for England, and a grateful governor let them turn Port Royal into their headquarters – hence 'the wickedest city in the world'.

Below: *The tomb of Lewis Galdy, who survived the Port Royal earthquake.*

At war at various times with the Netherlands, France and Spain, the British authorities turned a blind eye to the buccaneers of Port Royal – as long as they attacked only foreign shipping. Many of the pirates became extremely wealthy and some even respectable, like **Henry Morgan** (1635–88), whose buccaneer career was crowned by a knighthood and the governorship of the island of Jamaica.

Port Royal's glory days ended 7 June 1692, however, when it was struck by a severe earthquake, followed by tidal waves which inundated most of the city.

Above: *Sugar cultivation and slavery went hand in hand for centuries.*

Sugar and Slaves

By the 18th century, Europeans had recognised that the wealth of the Caribbean was not in gold but in **sugar**, which could be grown in huge quantities on the uncultivated soil of Jamaica and which commanded high prices in Europe, where there was an insatiable market. By the time of the British settlement, the Arawaks had already been almost annihilated. Attempts to work the cane-fields using indentured European labourers and Irish, Scottish and English **prisoners** of various civil wars and rebellions proved impracticable, as most quickly fell victim to disease. The solution was to import huge numbers of **slaves** from **West Africa**, ushering in one of the most shameful eras of oppression in history.

Sugar boomed, and Jamaica became one of the richest farming colonies. But the cost of human life for this new wealth was immense. During the 18th century more than 600,000 slaves were brought to Jamaica. One in five died

---

SUGAR

The British started growing sugar in **Barbados**, but the conquest of Jamaica opened up a new frontier of unimaginable wealth. By the 1740s there were almost 500 sugar plantations on the island and Jamaica was the world's biggest sugar producer.

during the Atlantic crossing, and Africans fell victim to local diseases as easily as Europeans. For every child born in slavery, six slaves died. Not surprisingly, slaves frequently sought to escape the brutal life on the plantations and succeeded in reaching freedom in the jungle fortresses of Maroon territory. Punishments for disobedience or attempted escape were unimaginably vicious, and execution by torture was routine. But life as a slave was so grim that even the most savage penalties failed to prevent repeated rebellions.

The fiercely independent Maroons remained a thorn in the side of the British. As early as 1690, they joined forces with rebel slaves in an island-wide rising that became known as the **First Maroon War**. The rebellion started among the slaves of the Clarendon area, most of whom were **Coromantee** from what is now Ghana. With the help of his brothers, **Accompong** and **Johnny**, and other Maroon chiefs such as **Cuffee** and **Quao**, the charismatic leader **Cudjoe** led a resistance for almost half a century. Eventually, the British brought in Indian trackers from the Mosquito Coast of Central America. One by one the Maroon villages were discovered and homes and fields burnt. On 31 March 1739, Cudjoe signed a treaty of friendship which set aside 1500 acres of land for the Maroons, and confirmed Cudjoe and his brothers as their rulers under the British crown, but bound them to return escaped slaves and to support the British against slave rebellions.

There were, however, subsequent slave rebellions. In 1760, a Coromantee leader named **Tacky** led hundreds of slaves in a revolt which proved hard to quell – even with the help of the Maroons – and there were many smaller risings. In 1795 there was a second war with the Maroons, sparked by the flogging of two Maroons for stealing a pig. The war lasted for six months until the governor, the Earl of Balcarres, brought in a contingent of killer dogs and their handlers from Cuba. Defeated, 600 Maroons were deported to Nova Scotia and, although those who remained were treated fairly leniently, Maroon power was finally broken.

> **MARCUS MOSIAH GARVEY**
>
> Marcus Mosiah Garvey (1887–1940) founded his **Universal Negro Improvement Association** to give the descendants of African slaves a new pride in their African roots, calling for Africans in the Caribbean and the Americas, and in the European colonies in Africa, to unite and rely on each other, not on whites. Urging African-Americans to go back to Africa to try to build a new world there, Garvey tried to set up his own ocean liner company, the **Black Star Line**, but his search for investors led to his imprisonment for mail fraud – almost certainly unjustly. He died in exile in London, but is buried in Jamaica, where he is a national hero.

Below: *A statue at St Ann's Bay of black leader Marcus Garvey.*

SLAVERY

Growing, harvesting and processing sugar cane is still brutally hard work, and in the 18th and 19th centuries, before mechanisation, was even harder – so hard, in fact, that no volunteer labour could be found. Sugar in industrial quantities could not be profitably produced with free labour. The plantations give the lie to the proverb that 'hard work never killed anybody' – it killed hundreds of thousands of slaves. In the end, the abolition of slavery was largely driven by economics and politics. Demand for sugar was down, the price had dropped, and the plantation lobby's political influence was in eclipse. Freedom for a slave, however, rarely meant freedom from want. For many, life after emancipation remained just as hard.

Below: *Sam Sharpe leads 20,000 slaves in the rebellion of 1831.*

Abolition

The beginning of the end of the dark era of slavery came in 1807, when Britain not only abolished British trade in slaves from Africa but set out to end the trade entirely. But the strength of the sugar lobby in Parliament and the conviction that the sugar plantations could be worked only by slave labour helped slavery survive in Jamaica until 1834.

The demise of slavery was hastened by the massive slave revolt of December 1831. Led by a Baptist minister named **Sam 'Daddy' Sharpe**, some 20,000 slaves rose in the Montego Bay area. They were persuaded to surrender peacefully when the British governor prematurely announced that slavery had been abolished by Parliament, but Sharpe and more than 1000 of his followers were nevertheless executed. Public opinion in Britain, which by then was strongly against slavery, was outraged and in 1834 slavery was finally abolished by Act of Parliament.

After Slavery

In some ways, life was even harder for black Jamaicans after abolition. Plantation owners no longer had the power to flog and torture at will, but all political and economic power remained in the hands of a tiny white ruling class. Though free, former slaves had to find shelter and sustenance for themselves, and there were few jobs outside the plantations, where many former slaves found themselves working for tiny wages under conditions not much better than those experienced during the days of slavery. Poverty was widespread and was made harsher by the American Civil War, when the southern states – which supplied much of Jamaica's food – were blockaded by the US Navy.

In October 1865, hunger and social injustice prompted the **Morant Bay Rebellion** by black Jamaicans demanding fairer treatment. The uprising was crushed with the usual savagery: some 430 rebels were hanged, hundreds more were flogged, and the leaders, **George William Gordon** and **Paul Bogle**, executed for treason. Both are today national heroes.

Above: *A mural in Morant Bay depicts the brutal ending of the 1865 uprising.*

However, the Morant Bay Rebellion had one positive result, persuading the white planters who ran the ruling Assembly to accept a slightly more enlightened Crown Colony government. Through the later 1800s, British governors reformed Jamaica's political and judicial systems, created a modern police force on British lines, and introduced minimum standards of health, education and welfare. Sugar was no longer all-important, and banana growing – which began in the late 19th century – quickly became a major part of the economy. Nevertheless, from the point of view of most Jamaicans, the colony remained a place of great economic, political and racial inequality.

The world depression of the 1930s brought even greater hardship and triggered island-wide riots. From this period of dissatisfaction emerged Jamaica's first home-grown political and workers' movements. **Alexander Bustamante's Industrial Trade Union** later spawned the centre-right **Jamaica Labour Party** (JLP). On the political left, **Norman Manley** founded the socialist **People's National Party** (PNP), which came to be allied to the **Jamaica Trades Union Congress** and the **National Workers' Union**. From the early '40s these rival movements were in the vanguard of the broad campaign for better pay and conditions, wider political rights for Jamaicans, and eventual full independence. In 1944 voting rights were given to all adults.

GEORGE GORDON

George William Gordon (1810–1865), son of a white farmer, was the first black Jamaican to be elected to Jamaica's colonial legislature. A lay preacher, he campaigned for the hundreds of thousands of Jamaicans left to fend for themselves after the end of the plantation system. He was caught up in the **Morant Bay Rebellion** of 1865, and executed as one of its leaders. Gordon appears to have been innocent, and his execution a convenient way of ridding the white ruling class of a thorn in its flesh. Today, like other historic resistance leaders including the Maroon chiefs **Nanny** and **Cudjoe**, **Paul Bogle** and **Sam Sharpe**, he is a national hero.

Above: *Montego Bay's airport is named after former leader Donald Sangster.*

Constitutional Change

Changes to the constitution in the 1950s culminated in internal self-government by an elected Jamaican cabinet in 1959, and in full independence on 6 August 1962. Jamaica's first free elections catapulted Alexander Bustamante and the JLP to power.

Firmly aligned with the capitalist world and committed to close ties with Britain and the Commonwealth, the JLP remained in power under Bustamante until 1967, and then for a further five years under his successors, **Donald Sangster** and **Hugh Shearer**. Eventually, the electorate decided it was time for a change. A rising population, ramshackle economy, poor infrastructure, urban and rural poverty, and high unemployment contributed to a landslide victory for the left-wing PNP in 1972. Led by **Michael Manley**, charismatic firebrand son of the PNP's founder, Jamaica moved closer to the non-aligned Third World, outlining ambitious plans for social reform. Sadly for Jamaica, the PNP achieved few of its aims despite almost a decade in power. Terrified by Manley's leftist rhetoric, foreign investors took their capital elsewhere, as did many better-off Jamaicans. The economy went into a nose-dive, foreign exchange reserves collapsed, and shortages of everyday goods became common. The US government, angry with the PNP's flirtation with socialist Cuba, painted Manley as a second Fidel Castro, and many on the left of Jamaican politics still see the hidden hand of destabilisation experts of the US Central Intelligence Agency behind the economic and political catastrophes of the 1970s.

The Modern Era

Political unrest increased until, at the end of the decade, Jamaica seemed on the verge of civil war. Large areas of Kingston's ghettoes appeared to be ruled by armed gangs pledging allegiance to either party and, despite a celebrated

---

UNCLE SAM'S BACKYARD

Cricket, the Commonwealth and the Queen notwithstanding, Jamaica is more influenced by the USA than Britain these days. **Miami**, after all, is only 90 minutes away by air, and Jamaican airwaves are dominated by American radio and TV stations. **Rock 'n roll** imported from the States helped create reggae, and black American role models as diverse as boxer **Mike Tyson** and Jamaican-born **General Colin Powell** are heroes to young Jamaicans. America has also taken a close interest in Jamaican affairs – sometimes too close for comfort. Many still believe the economic chaos and violence which toppled left-leaning government of **Michael Manley** at the end of the 1970s was orchestrated by the CIA.

plea for peace by reggae star **Bob Marley**, Michael Manley and JLP leader Edward Seaga, the violence continued. With hundreds dead by the time the JLP emerged as winner of the 1979 general election, the JLP's opponents argued that the decline in violence after the election implied that JLP supporters, not the PNP, had been the main culprits.

Seaga's government swung the economy through another U-turn, adopting the free-market principles of 'Reaganomics'. A more moderate PNP was returned to power in 1989 and has remained in government since. The PNP is now under the leadership of P.J. Patterson after Manley's retirement in 1993. The government has had to contend with continuing economic difficulty. In 1999 the island was paralysed by two days of rioting in protest against the latest in a long series of fuel tax increases. More positively, several factors from grassroots campaigns against violence in the cities as well as government initiatives seemed to be having an impact on levels of violent crimes in Kingston and elsewhere by the late 1990s.

> **TOURISM**
>
> Tourism came to Jamaica in the early 1900s when **Captain Lorenzo Dow Baker** realised he could bring visitors from chilly North America to **Port Antonio** in his fleet of banana boats. World War II put Europe off-limits to wealthy Americans, making Jamaica even more popular. After the war, tourism flourished, but took a dip with the political violence of the '70s. Recovery began as cheaper flights brought new waves of visitors from Europe. All-inclusive resorts, conceived in the '80s, have since boomed, offering security and value for money – but mostly cocooning their guests from the real Jamaica.

GOVERNMENT AND ECONOMY

Jamaica is a member of the Commonwealth, with its own constitution and political institutions. A two-chamber **Parliament** consists of an elected **House of Representatives** and a **Senate** whose members are jointly appointed by the prime minister and the leader of the opposition. Elections are held every five years, but Queen Elizabeth II remains ceremonial head of state, represented by a governor-general who is traditionally a distinguished Jamaican appointed by the prime minister. At local government level, Jamaica

Below: *A cruise ship lies off Ocho Rios, a hub of tourism in Jamaica.*

> **NATIONAL STATISTICS**
>
> Around 40 per cent of Jamaica's **population** lives in the four major cities – **Kingston**, **Montego Bay**, **Spanish Town**, and **Mandeville**, with the remainder living in rural areas. More than 700,000 people live in Kingston and 100,000 in Mo Bay. **Unemployment** averages 25 per cent and youth unemployment is virtually 100 per cent in the poorest of the Kingston ghettoes. Jamaica is a young country, with two in three Jamaicans less than 29 years old.

is divided into three counties (Cornwall, Middlesex and Surrey) and these, in turn, are divided into a total of 14 **parishes** – all with distinctly English names – which are administered by elected councils. Jamaica is a strongly partisan country, and political grumbling is part of the Jamaican way of life, with supporters of each side frequently and vocally accusing rival politicos of corruption, fraud, cynicism and incompetence.

Economic Development

A generation after independence, Jamaica's economy is still one of the most unbalanced in the world, with a huge proportion of income and wealth in the hands of a relatively tiny number of people. **Emigration** remains a perennial problem, as many Jamaicans leave to seek a better living overseas, especially in the US, Canada and the UK. **Unemployment** is also cripplingly high, averaging about 25 per cent, and almost 100 per cent in some of the poorest parts of Kingston.

Industry and Agriculture

Opposite: *Though illegal, marijuana plantations are not an unusual sight.*
Below: *Bauxite ore is loaded on to a freighter at Discovery Bay.*

Tourism is the country's biggest foreign currency earner and one of its major employers, with an annual turnover of close to US$ 900 million. Many Jamaicans are ambivalent about the holiday industry. Although they recognise that it brings much-needed cash and jobs, they object to being treated as a nation of waiters, bar staff and taxi-drivers. Second to tourism is **bauxite mining**, with bauxite ore bringing in around 40 per cent of export earnings.

Sugar cane is the most important crop and the country's biggest employer, but **bananas**, **cocoa**

THE PEOPLE

and **coffee** are also rather important revenue earners. **Wages** for this kind of work are low, and many people earn as little as US$20 a week. Imported and manufactured goods are expensive, even by British or US standards. Jamaica must import all its **fuel** and, as the Jamaican dollar declines steadily against the US dollar, this only adds to the country's economic problems.

Since the early 1980s, Jamaican authorities have tacitly – and sometimes openly – admitted that the illegal trade in **ganja** (marijuana) has become an important part of the economy. In Jamaica's steamy tropical climate, ganja grows profusely even on poor soil which will support no other cash crops. Some sources have estimated that the ganja business is worth as much as US$1 billion a year, outstripping all legitimate sectors of the economy. Arguably, legalisation could bring the country's economic woes to an end overnight, but the predictably violent reaction from the US precludes any such move.

THE PEOPLE

One in three of Jamaica's 2.5 million people lives in Kingston, with around 260,000 scattered around the island's other main towns and villages. Around 95 per cent of Jamaicans are black descendants of **African** slaves, although skin tones range from very dark to very light, and there are small **Indian**, **Lebanese** and **Chinese** minorities. Since the tourist-deterring troubles of the late 1970s, the Jamaican Tourist Board has spent millions

---

COFFEE

Jamaica produces the world's finest – and most expensive coffee. On the slopes of the **Blue Mountains**, some 4000 farms produce up to 15,000 bushels of Blue Mountain beans a year. The arabica coffee grown here originated in **Ethiopia** and was brought over via **Martinique** in 1728. Today, the right to use the Blue Mountain name is strictly controlled, with the best of the crop grown above the 2000ft (6560m) mark. But you'll be lucky to be served Blue Mountain coffee in Jamaica – almost all is exported to Japan, where it fetches incredibly high prices.

> **JAMAICANS OVERSEAS**
>
> A combination of poverty, energy and high aspirations has driven many Jamaicans overseas in search of better jobs and living conditions than they find at home. There are large communities of first-, second- and third-generation Jamaicans in the UK, the USA and Canada, and nearer to home several thousand Jamaicans work in the Cayman Islands. Many are high achievers in their adopted homes, not only as musicians and athletes – traditional routes out of the ghetto – but as professionals, statesmen and even military supremos such as **General Colin Powell**, former head of the US Chiefs of Staff.

Below: *Sunday worship is a regular occasion in this church-going society.*

stressing the warmth and friendliness of the Jamaican people. On first acquaintance, though, most visitors find Jamaicans rather more reserved than initially imagined. Eliciting a smile from a Jamaican barman, bank teller or shop assistant is an achievement. Sometimes, it can be as difficult to attract the attention of a waiter as to avoid the attentions of beach hustlers, black-market money changers and small-time drug dealers, all of whom may become abusive if you politely refuse their offers.

The huge gap between your disposable income and that of the Jamaicans who serve you accounts, for a large part, for this behaviour. That said, many visitors perceive Jamaicans as aggressive simply because of the direct way they express themselves. A souvenir pedlar is more likely to seek your attention with 'You! Come 'ere!' than with a polite 'Excuse me'.

Language

Although Jamaica's language is officially **English**, it takes no more than a few sentences for the visitor to realise that Jamaican **patois** is quite different from any other Anglo-Saxon dialect. Jamaicans are comfortable in both 'standard' English – flavoured with American and British influences – and their own spicy, incomprehensible dialect. The richly creative Jamaican patois is still evolving, with its own distinct grammar and syntax, and its vocabulary features numerous loan-words from West African languages and other sources as disparate as Gaelic, Spanish and 17th-century English. Patois is clearly on its way to becoming an authentic language in its own right, and there are serious proposals that the Jamaican government should recognise the language as a second national language.

Religion

Jamaican life juxtaposes a bawdy tolerance with a dignified conservatism. On the one hand, it is common for both men and women to have children by several partners; there are more ganja smokers than abstainers; and the 'slack' verses of today's reggae and dub musicians revel in explicit sexual detail. On the other hand, every settlement – no matter how tiny – has at least one church, and Sunday worship is an occasion for formal wear and staid behaviour – no matter how raucous the preceding Saturday night. The **Anglican Church of Jamaica** is the most widespread denomination, with substantial numbers of **Roman Catholic** worshippers and a myriad of smaller **Protestant** churches.

Jamaica's unique home-grown religion, **Rastafarianism**, is a rather complicated brew of Old Testament Christianity, ganja-fuelled mysticism, revealed truth and back-to-Africa fundamentalism. 'Rastas' wear their hair in long, matted dreadlocks, venerate the former Emperor of Ethiopia, **Haile Selassie**, and aim to live a contemplative life away from the temptations and tribulations of the modern, urban 'Babylon'. It is a major religion in Jamaica and includes various sects. Some followers have even emigrated to Ethiopia, regarded as the source of their religion. But, at times, true Rastafarians may seem to be outnumbered by those for whom the lion-like mane is a style statement rather than the expression of a deeply held belief.

Above: *A Kingstonian takes time out to enjoy a welcome cool beer.*

OBEAH

In Haiti it's called **voodoo**, in the Dominican Republic **santeria**, and in Jamaica it is known as **obeah**. Under any name, it is a surviving, much-altered relic of the original animist religions of West Africa, with its practitioners appealing to a host of deities to intercede on their behalf. Brought over and covertly maintained by African slaves and their descendants well into the mid-19th century, obeah is said to be used clandestinely to this day, to bring both good and bad luck.

Art and Culture

Like many fledgling nations, Jamaica took time to find its artistic feet. Until well into the 20th century, the cultural roots of the majority of its people were ignored, suppressed, or regarded as second-rate, and the imported European traditions of the white plantocracy prevailed. From the 1920s onwards, though, a truly Jamaican artistic movement was born. The works of many of its founders can be seen today in the National Gallery of Jamaica in Kingston, perhaps the finest art collection in the Caribbean region, and paintings and carvings by their successors can be bought at excellent private galleries in Kingston and all over the island. Look out for works by the late **Edna Manley** (wife of PNP founder Norman Manley and mother of the former prime minister Michael Manley), whose powerful carvings – many of them with strong political and social messages – put her at the forefront of this Jamaican cultural revolution. One of her last works, *The Voice*, is a tribute to the late Bob Marley, the man who brought Jamaica's own music to the world stage.

Truly original artists from this first new wave of Jamaican creativity include **Shepherd Kapo**, whose powerful, quasi-religious paintings of visions and illusionary landscapes as well as his remarkable carvings adorn their own section of the National Gallery; the naturalistic painter **Albert Huie**; and the sculptor **Alvin Marriott**. In 1950, the **Jamaica School**

PUNCTUALITY

Jamaica is as relaxed about punctuality as about most other things. Very little happens exactly when it is supposed to – though **Air Jamaica** is succeeding in sticking closer to its schedule since privatisation. Along with 'no problem', 'soon come' is one of the most overused – and inaccurate – phrases in the island's vocabulary. There is nothing you can do about this, so lay back and enjoy it. What's the hurry? You're in Jamaica, mon!

THE PEOPLE

of Art was set up to become the nexus for development of a Jamaican artistic tradition, and in 1976 it became part of the newly created **Kingston Cultural Training Centre**, which comprises schools of art, music, dance and drama.

As well as the work of its mainstream artists, Jamaica abounds in talented, self-taught artists whose carvings and colourful paintings can be bought at very affordable prices in galleries and craft markets around the island's main resorts. Naive and imitative though these works often are, the best of them radiate a brilliance of colour and a raw, youthful energy that is truly Jamaican, and make excellent souvenirs of your Jamaican holiday.

Music

Music is probably Jamaica's best-known export. Since stars like **Jimmy Cliff**, **Toots and The Maytals** and, above all, **Bob Marley and The Wailers**, took **reggae** out of the ghetto and into the world album charts more than 20 years ago, the distinctive, rather slow-moving beat and throbbing bass of Jamaican music have travelled the world. Reggae emerged in the early 1970s (**Frederick Hibbert** of Toots and The Maytals is credited with inventing the name), the latest mutation in a long line of descent from traditional melodies and rhythms brought to Jamaica by enslaved Africans.

Deprived of material possessions and robbed of their native languages and traditions – and even of their names – music was the only memory of Africa the slaves could keep, and must have been especially precious.

African rhythms contributed to the invention of the slow and sensual musical

> **ETHNIC MIX**
>
> Most Jamaicans are of mixed European descent, though the **Maroons** have a proud, almost pure African pedigree. During the 18th and 19th centuries, there was a finely graduated scale of distinctions, depending on one's ratio of white to African blood. With the end of slavery, African-Jamaicans were understandably reluctant to go on working on the plantations, and Asian and Chinese indentured labourers were brought in. Some of their descendants are still here, as are the descendants of the 'Syrian' – actually mostly Lebanese – traders who came to try their luck in the last century.

Opposite: *Colourful designs like this batik hoopoe bird are common.*
Below: *Dreadlocks and reggae are both distinctive Jamaican exports.*

Above: *Slick entertainment at the Grand Lido resort near Negril.*

style called **mento** which reigned supreme until the 1950s, when the sound of the USA started to dominate Jamaican airwaves. Influenced by jazz, rhythm and blues drifting over the Caribbean from New Orleans and points north, Jamaican musicians invented their own variation on the theme. This they called **ska**, a rather fast-moving, mostly instrumental dance rhythm which was subsequently carried to Britain by migrant Jamaicans. But it was reggae, evolving out of ska by way of a slower sound called 'rock steady', that really caught the world's imagination.

Reggae's first exponents included established musicians such as Frederick 'Toots' Hibbert, Jimmy Cliff and **Desmond Decker**. However, it took four boys from the streets of Kingston's Trench Town ghetto to take reggae worldwide.

As the Wailing Rude Boys – and later The Wailers – **Bob Marley**, **Bunny 'Wailer' Livingstone**, **Peter 'Tosh' MacIntosh** and **Junior Braithwaite** wrote and performed their own songs, many of them expressing discontent and protest, that struck a chord not only in Jamaica but worldwide. And you could dance to them. In the mid-1970s reggae exploded onto the international music scene and began to influence established jazz and rock musicians all over the world. Since then it has never gone away.

Reggae's current exponents keep the flame alight, while Jamaican music continued its evolution into forms like **dancehall**, with its 'chattering' DJ's interacting with their audiences, and **ragga**. (ragamuffin), both of which owe an enormous debt to reggae.

PATOIS

To the untrained ear, Jamaican patois does not sound even faintly like English. Most Jamaicans, whether fishermen, farmers or Harvard-trained businessmen, switch fluently from Caribbean-accented standard English when talking to foreigners into their own impenetrable dialect when talking to each other, and for many younger middle-class Jamaicans fluency in the patois is essential to their street credibility. Long neglected and even looked down upon, patois is beginning to receive recognition as both a language in its own right and central to the nation's culture, with many Jamaican **poets** and **authors** following in the footsteps of **reggae** musicians to use it in their own work.

Film

Fabulous landscapes, perfect weather, close proximity to the USA and a long tradition of tax breaks for foreign film production companies have made Jamaica a favourite location for many well-loved movies, from the golden years of Hollywood (when, led by Errol Flynn, many stars sojourned on the island) to the heyday of the James Bond films (Bond's creator, Ian Fleming, had a home near Ocho Rios). Home-made films starring Jamaican artists are fewer, but one in particular deserves mention because it played a big part in launching reggae onto the world stage. *The Harder They Come*, starring musician Jimmy Cliff as a fiercely ambitious ghetto kid bent on fame, and with an exhaustive soundtrack featuring tracks by Cliff, The Maytals, and Desmond Decker, remains a cult classic. Other home-grown movies include the odd offering, *Countryman*, a tale of ganja, corruption and Rasta mysticism set against the political violence of the late 1970s, and the acclaimed comedy *Cool Runnings*, the unlikely tale of a team of young Jamaicans bent on bobsleigh victory in the Winter Olympics.

BOB MARLEY

Robert Nesta Marley (1940–81) took Jamaican **reggae** music to a world audience. Born at **Nine Mile**, near Runaway Bay, he moved with his family to the **Trench Town** ghetto area of Kingston at 13. By his late teens he was already making music, with a band called **The Wailers**. Though his fellow-Wailers were fine musicians, Marley's song-writing flair and soaring voice lifted the band above the run-of-the-mill competition. In 1978, Marley was shot by four gunmen at his Kingston home, but survived to host a concert which brought prime minister Michael Manley and opposition leader Eddie Seaga together to urge – unsuccessfully – an end to the current violence. His death from brain cancer was tragically early.

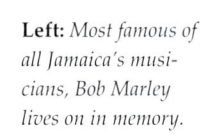

Sport and Recreation

Jamaicans – and its men especially – take an enthusiastic interest in sport. **Cricket** is a runaway favourite, and Jamaicans follow the fortunes of national players and the West Indies team with near-religious fervour. When a major match is in progress, local bars that are usually noisy with the sound of dominoes, reggae and political discussion are silent except for the voice of the radio commentator. Every town, and almost every village, has its own cricket pitch, and you're likely to see cricket matches in progress any time and anywhere. The teams may be in immaculate whites on a suitably immaculate parish ground, or equally made up of barefoot

Left: *Most famous of all Jamaica's musicians, Bob Marley lives on in memory.*

INTRODUCING JAMAICA

CRICKET

Cricket is more than a national pastime in Jamaica; it's a national obsession. Thousands pack Kingston's **Sabina Park** when Jamaica plays other Caribbean nations, or when the **West Indies** meets England, Australia, New Zealand or South Africa. Jamaican boys have bat and ball in hand as soon as they can walk, and any piece of flat ground in town or village is used as a makeshift pitch as soon as school or church is out. In a nation which lives in the shadow of the US and which is still inventing its own identity, cricket is the most visible and longest lasting link of Jamaica's links with the UK, and even the flood of US sports such as baseball, basketball and gridiron football on satellite television show little sign of dimming Jamaica's passionate love affair with cricket.

village kids dressed only in ragged shorts, playing with an assortment of makeshift equipment.

Soccer is an even more popular everyday pastime, though it does not feature high on Jamaica's sporting calendar as an organised sport and Jamaica has only just begun to make its mark internationally.

For the visitor, Jamaica is a holiday destination rich in sporting activities, ranging from **golf** on some of the world's top courses – such as Tryall, home of golf's biggest prize event, the World Championship – to **tennis**, **riding**, **deep-sea fishing** for marlin, wahoo and tuna, and a wide range of **watersports**.

Right: *Immensely popular with divers from around the world, the Caribbean's waters are warm and teem with marine life such as silversides; top of the list of places to dive is almost certainly the Cayman Islands, but Jamaica's coastline also includes several stretches of healthy coral reef.*

THE PEOPLE

Food and Drink

Jamaica's culinary tradition is heavy on calories and even heavier on spicy flavourings. But be sure to sample **jerk** chicken, beef, pork or fish – marinated in a piquant mix of hot peppers, pimento, spices, thyme, and onions, and grilled over fragrant barbecue coals of allspice wood. Equally spicy is **curry goat**, eaten with rice on special occasions, or meat-filled **Jamaica patties** stuffed with flavoured chicken or beef mince. Kidney beans (known as 'red peas') appear in **red pea soup**, a blend of beef, beans, and onions flavoured with peppers, thyme and garlic, and in **red peas and rice**, the Jamaican chef's favourite filler. **Ackee**, a red, pod-like fruit which when cooked is almost indistinguishable from perfectly scrambled egg, is usually flavoured with salt cod, another Jamaican favourite, or bacon. Other vegetables include **calalloo**, a spinach-like leaf served as a side dish or in **pepperpot soup**, which also features yam, peppers, coconut milk, and beef. Delicious fruit includes **pineapple**, star apple **sweetsop** and, of course, **coconut**, the milk of which is an essential ingredient in dozens of delicious cocktails. **Jamaican rum**, distilled from sugar cane by makers including the Appleton and Wray & Nephew distilleries, is renowned for its subtle potency. Gold rum, aged in oak barrels, can be mellow enough to sip after dinner, while white rum is more suitable with mixers or as a base for cocktails. Jamaican overproof rum, with a proof rating of up to 140 degrees, is arguably more suitable for use as rocket fuel than as a drink. Coffee-flavoured **Tia Maria** liqueur, another Jamaican original, is a delicious after-dinner drink, while on a hot afternoon on the beach an ice-cold **Red Stripe** lager, brewed by Desnoes and Geddes, is guaranteed to hit the spot.

Above: *Jerk chicken, grilled corn and watermelon feature in a platter.*

JAMAICAN DISHES

Everybody has to try **jerk**, but there are lots of other Jamaican dishes on the menu. Try **festival**, a fried cornmeal dumpling, or **breadfruit** – boiled or roasted – to go with your jerk meat. **Bammy**, a round flat bread made from grated cassava (a yam-like root from South America) goes well with fish. **Johnny cakes** are fried dumplings, **callaloo** is a spinach-like vegetable, and **patties** – pitta-like meat pies stuffed with spicy beef, chicken or fish – are a meal in themselves. If you are wondering what gives Jamaican jerk seasoning its legendary bite, the culprit is 'scotch bonnet' – one of the most formidable chile peppers to be found.

2
Kingston and St Andrew

Jamaica's capital lies on the south coast and boasts one of the most striking locations of any city in the world. Kingston stretches inland from the **Caribbean** towards the spectacular inland scenery of the **Blue Mountains**, which dominate the capital's northern skyline. A sprawling urban centre of more than 800,000 people – almost one-third of Jamaica's total population – Kingston seems to have little in common with the laid-back resorts on the island's best beaches, or with the small fishing villages of Jamaica's coasts and mountains.

Kingston is Jamaica's second capital. The first, **Spanish Town** – centre of the first Spanish settlement – lies some 10 miles (16km) west of Kingston, and is likely to be eventually absorbed by Kingston's urban sprawl. **Port Royal**, the infamous buccaneer's lair which was demolished by a giant earthquake in 1692, lies just across Kingston Harbour and can be seen from the Kingston waterfront.

As your plane makes its approach into **Norman Manley International Airport** it is easy to see why Spaniards, pirates and British governors favoured this part of the island. The airport is located on a long spur of land which stretches from the mainland, with Port Royal at its western tip. **Kingston Harbour**, sheltered by this narrow peninsula, is the finest anchorage in the Caribbean, and one of the largest natural harbours in the world – which is precisely why successive occupiers made this area their Caribbean headquarters, and why rival powers such as France so keenly sought to evict the British from Jamaica.

CARIBBEAN SEA

Don't Miss

*** **Bob Marley Museum:** celebrates the life of the godfather of reggae.
*** **Devon House:** restored mansion built by Jamaica's first black millionaire.
** **Port Royal:** relics of the bloody heyday of piracy on the Spanish Main.
** **Crafts Market:** colourful shopping on Kingston's waterfront.

Opposite: *Devon House is one of Jamaica's finest buildings.*

> **CLIMATE**
>
> Kingston can get very **hot**. Coastal temperatures tend to average 28°C (82°F), with a maximum of 32°C (90°F) and a minimum of 27°C (49°F). Although the south coast generally receives less rain than the north, there is always the possibility of tropical storms and downpours during July–October.

Kingston was founded in the early 1690s, following the destruction of Port Royal, but became the capital only in 1872, when the seat of government was relocated from Spanish Town. Successive fires, and another earthquake in 1907, have left relatively few older buildings standing amid more recent residential and commercial building, most of it constructed from the 1950s and '60s onward.

Kingston has a throbbing street life, with busy markets (almost every downtown street has 'higglers' or street vendors) and an even hotter nightlife.

Cultural venues include the 1000-seat **Ward Theatre** and also the 600-seat **Little Theatre**, which host performances by the **National Dance Theatre Company**, the **National Chorale** and the **Jamaica Philharmonic Symphony Orchestra** as well as reggae which may be heard in dozens of the city's night-spots.

North of the city, where the foothills of the Blue Mountains offer cooling breezes, plush residential suburbs house some of Kingston's wealthier residents. Straddling St Andrew, Portland and St Thomas parishes, the **Blue Mountains** rise to a height of 7402ft (2256m). The marvellous Blue Mountains–John Crow Mountains national parks offer a growing network of hiking trails.

DOWNTOWN KINGSTON

Many of Kingston's oldest colonial buildings and landmarks, as well as a string of modern banks, corporate headquarters and several of the city's main tourist attractions, are close to the harbour waterfront. There also two museums of note.

National Gallery ***

Situated in the Roy West Building at Kingston Hall, the National Gallery's collection includes pieces by artists such as **Joseph Kidd** and **George Robertson**, whose work comprises portraits of governors, generals and wealthy planters of the colonial era as well as island landscapes. These, however, are outshone by the much more vital and exciting works of 20th-century Jamaican artists, notably the outstanding sculptures of **Edna Manley**. A common theme in Manley's work is the need for Jamaicans to feel dignity and pride in themselves, from works like *The Diggers*, dating from the 1930s, to the powerful depiction of Bob Marley, *The Voice*, which has pride of place, guitar in one hand and finger pointed heavenward. The gallery also has a fine collection of the work of the revivalist painter and woodcarver **Shepherd Kapo**. Also worth looking out for are the works of artists such as **Leonard Daley**, **Albert Artwell**, and **Everald Brown** who have taken much of their inspiration from Rastafarianism. Open Monday–Thursday from 11:00–15:30 and Friday from 11:00–16:00.

Institute of Jamaica (and African Caribbean Institute) *

At 12–16 East Street is this collection of tools, utensils, musical instruments and other artefacts which cast a rather interesting sidelight on Jamaican history from the point of view of its

> **DANCE COMPANIES**
>
> Kingston has several dance companies. **The National Dance Theatre Company** has won international acclaim for its interpretations of Jamaican traditional and modern forms. Other outstanding exponents of Jamaican dance – an exciting blend of Africa and Europe that is uniquely Jamaican – are LACADCO (**Latin American and Caribbean Dance Company**), as well as **Movements** and **Jayteens**, all of which perform regularly at venues in the capital and around the island.

Below: *Ocean Boulevard contains a string of corporate headquarters, and the National Gallery.*

> **HIGGLERS AND HUSTLERS**
>
> For many, if not most Jamaicans, life is a matter of making it as best you can, and the crowds of **hustlers** who greet you as soon as you step into the airport arrivals hall are prime examples of the Jamaican hustler, who you'll meet at every turn offering a range of goods and services from straw hats and parasail rides to transportation and illicit substances. They can persist, but a firm but polite refusal will eventually deter them. **Higglers** – the stalwart ladies who dominate most Jamaican marketplaces – are worthy adversaries for even the most skilled negotiator, and you'll be lucky to get the better of the amiable bargaining involved in buying anything from them.

African Caribbean people. Founded in 1879, the Institute also houses Jamaica's national **archives**, with the largest **reference library** documenting the history of the Caribbean anywhere in the world. The Institute is at the very heart of Jamaica's cultural scene, housing the **Cultural Training Centre**, which includes the national schools of art, dance and drama, and the **African Caribbean Institute**, a centre for research into cultural and traditional links between Africa and Jamaica and other Caribbean nations. Open from Monday–Friday between 09:00–16:00.

Crafts Market **

On the waterfront at Port Royal Street, the crafts market offers typical Jamaican souvenir shopping. Best buys include linens, silk and cotton batik **textiles**, **wood carvings**, colourful woven **baskets** and vibrant naive **paintings** of rural and urban life. That said, the Kingston market is far from unique. There are very similar crafts markets at other resort centres, including Negril, Montego Bay and Ocho Rios, so if you are staying elsewhere on the island and your time in Kingston is limited, you may want to give this market a fairly low priority. Open 09:00–17:00 daily.

Kingston Parish Church **

The original Kingston Parish Church on the corner of King Street and South Parade was built in the late 17th century, as indicated by a tombstone in its churchyard dated 1699. Destroyed in the 1907 earthquake, the 1911 building which now stands in its place is a copy of the original building. Just like London's Cockneys, city-dwellers claim that the only true Kingstonians – a breed now heavily outnumbered by migrants from the countryside – are people born 'under the clock', or within earshot of the Parish Church bell. The bell is housed in a square

NEW KINGSTON AND OLD HOPE ROAD

clocktower, and was cast for the first Parish Church in 1715, surprisingly surviving the earthquake. Open daily.

Ward Theatre **

On the Parade on the north side of the pleasant William Grant Park stands the impressive Ward Theatre. Its pale blue-and-white colonial baroque frontage makes this one of Kingston's most attractive older buildings. Given to the city by **Colonel Charles Ward**, it opened in 1911 and is now a venue for the **National Dance Theatre Company**, whose lively performances are well worth watching, and for a number of amateur theatre companies.

Gordon House *

Built in 1960, Gordon House is named after **George William Gordon**, who was executed after the Morant Bay rebellion of 1865 and is now remembered as one of Jamaica's most prominent national heroes. It is the seat of Jamaica's **House of Representatives**, and British visitors in particular will notice a close resemblance to the interior design and protocol of Westminster Palace's House of Commons – though the resemblance does not extend to the building's exterior. Visits are by appointment only.

NEW KINGSTON AND OLD HOPE ROAD

Between Hope Road and Old Hope Road lies New Kingston, home to most of the city's international hotels. The area also contains a fair number of embassies, government buildings and offices. To the east along the Old Hope Road are the historic Hope Botanical Gardens.

Above: *The pool at the Wyndham Hotel provides a luxury refuge.*
Opposite: *A young stallholder at the Kingston crafts market brandishes Bob Marley shirts for sale.*

BRITISH RELICS

Jamaica is completely independent of the UK, but relics of British rule abound, from elderly British-made **Morris** and **Oxford** cars still clanking around the streets of Kingston (and driving on the left) to the grand ceremonial which surrounds the office of **Governor General** or the British military-style dress uniforms worn by **Jamaican policemen**, complete with broad red stripe down the side of the trousers. The portrait of **Queen Elizabeth II** on every Jamaican dollar and cent is another reminder of links with the colonial power.

Above: *Built for Jamaica's earliest black millionaire, Devon House has an interesting history.*

HALF WAY TREE

All over Jamaica you will see the towering **kapok** tree, easily identified by the fluffy white fibres (used for stuffing cushions and soft furnishings) which explode from its seed pods. In central Kingston, **Half Way Tree** marks the spot where one mighty specimen became a landmark for early settlers. Once midway between Kingston and the market gardens of the nearby hills, it is now in the very heart of the urban sprawl.

Devon House ★★★

This immaculately restored mansion at 26 Hope Road dates from 1881, when it was built for Jamaica's first black millionaire, the shipwright **George Stiebel**. Stiebel's fortune was made not in Jamaica, where people of African descent were still at a great disadvantage during the 19th century, but in South America, and the elegant home he commissioned on his return was clearly designed to show off his hard-earned wealth to the greatest advantage. Furnished with 19th-century antiques, the house, with its arcade of white pillars supporting a pretty first-floor balcony, is one of Jamaica's most handsome buildings. Its outbuildings now house some attractive arts, crafts and antique shops as well as two pleasant restaurants. Open 09:30–17:00 Tuesday–Saturday.

King's House and Jamaica House ★★

Massive wrought-iron gates just off Hope Road mark the entrance to the vast landscaped grounds which enclose **King's House**, residence of the Governor General, and Jamaica House, the executive office of the prime minister. The Governor General of Jamaica is the Queen's official representative on the island and is chosen by appointment from among the ranks of the island's dignitaries. King's House stands on the site of the Bishop's Lodge, the residence of the Bishop of Jamaica, which was destroyed in 1907 by an earthquake. Rebuilt to a design by the English architect Sir Charles Nicholson, it now has a grace and dignity which befit its role and is enhanced by the 200 acres of beautiful surrounding tropical gardens. King's House was refurbished from top to bottom in 1995–96 and is now a marvellous setting for its collections of antique furniture and paintings, including a portrait by Sir Joshuah Reynolds of King George III and portraits of other British monarchs. It is sometimes possible to take tea with the Governor General at King's House as a guest of the 'Meet the People' programme run by the Jamaica Tourist Board; contact the JTB for details. Open 09:00–17:00 Monday–Saturday.

Built in the 1960s as the premier's official residence, **Jamaica House** stands amid equally attractively landscaped grounds but is a rather less striking building. Jamaica House is not open to visitors.

Bob Marley Museum ★★★

No tour of the city is complete without a visit to the museum at 56 Hope Road dedicated to Kingston's most famous son. Bob Marley's home and the studio of his **Tuff Gong** record label are now a museum tracing his career from ghetto childhood to international megastar. High points of the one-hour guided tour include a look at Marley's platinum and

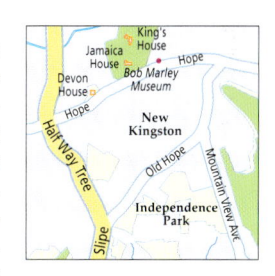

> **UNIVERSITY OF THE WEST INDIES**
>
> The **Kingston Campus** of the University of the West Indies, at **Mona**, is one of UWI's three campuses (the others are in Barbados and Trinidad) serving the 14 independent English-speaking nations of the Caribbean. The adjoining **University Hospital of the West Indies** is the Caribbean's premier teaching hospital.

Below: *The Bob Marley Museum is the city's most popular attraction.*

EARTHQUAKES

Earthquakes have punctuated Jamaican history, from the cataclysm which plunged **Port Royal** into the waters of the Caribbean in 1692 to relatively minor tremors. One survivor of the 1692 'quake was a certain **Mr Galdy**, who fell into an open crevasse only to be flung clear when it closed. This lucky man's grave can be seen in St Peter's churchyard, at Port Royal. Kingston was struck again in 1907, in a 'quake which demolished much of the city, leaving few of its older buildings undamaged.

---

gold discs, Rastafarian religious trappings, and the tree under which he liked to sit and smoke huge quantities of ganja (legend has it that the Marley household got through up to a pound of quality weed daily). There is also a 20-minute video compilation of Marley's greatest hits and live performances. Open 09:30–16.30 Monday, Tuesday, Thursday and Friday, 12:30–17:30 Wednesday, Saturday and holidays.

Hope Botanical Gardens

The **Hope Estate**, now the home of the largest botanical gardens in the Caribbean region, is among the oldest estates in Jamaica. It was founded by one of Oliver Cromwell's officers, **Major Richard Hope**, who came to the Caribbean with the Parliamentary army in 1655. The 200-acre (81ha) gardens, next to the Mona Campus of the **University of the West Indies**, were bought from the government by the Hope Estate in 1881 and declared Jamaica's Royal Botanical Gardens in 1953, on the coronation of Queen Elizabeth II and her visit that year to Jamaica. The once-grand gardens feature ornamental ponds, cactus garden, shrubberies and greenhouses but have lost their former glory. Open 09.00–17.30 daily.

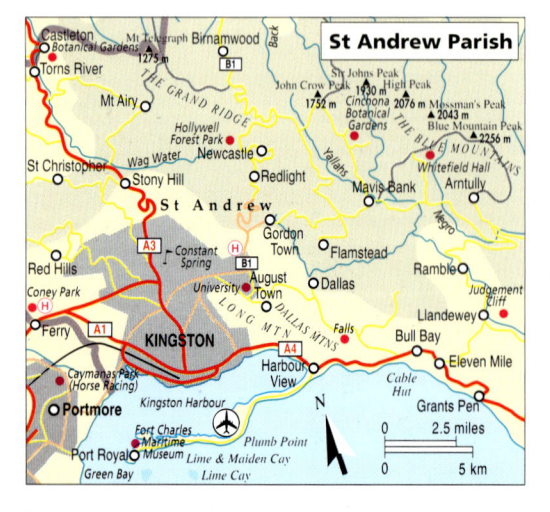

PORT ROYAL

There is little left at Port Royal to indicate that it was in its heyday known as 'the wickedest city in the world'. In the 17th century, this harbour city situated at the western end of the narrow, snake-like Palisadoes Peninsula which protects Kingston Harbour from the surf of the Caribbean was a safe haven for the most feared buccaneers of the Spanish Main – including men such as **Edward 'Blackbeard' Teach** (who ended his days on the executioner's gibbet) and **Henry Morgan** (who made good, was knighted by the Crown and became a Governor General of Jamaica). It was clearly no place for honest, law-abiding folk and, when the earthquake of 7 June 1692 swept most of Port Royal into the sea, there were plenty who were ready to see the catastrophe as divine judgment on the wicked ways of its inhabitants.

Above: *Port Royal was once the base for a group of buccaneers who made their living from attacking Spanish and other ships in the Caribbean.*

The Waterfront *

Today, the waterfront is a quiet fishing port (except, of course, at weekends when it attracts flocks of day-trippers from Kingston) with a handful of surviving 17th-, 18th- and 19th-century buildings to remind visitors of its glory days. Fishing pirogues and drying fishing nets line the waterside at **Fisherman's Beach**, just off Port Royal High Street.

There are ambitious plans to recreate Port Royal in the historical spirit of its pirating past, with more museums, shops and restaurants echoing a buccaneer theme, and already its historic buildings, two small museums and a veritable archipelago of offshore coral islets (perfect for swimming and snorkelling) make it worth the trip from central Kingston.

The drive to Port Royal takes you past the bobbing masts of the **Royal Jamaica Yacht Club** flotilla at anchor midway along the peninsula, and the runways of **Norman Manley International Airport**. Alternatively – and considerably more entertaining – take the ferry from Kingston's Pier 2, which leaves every two hours between 06:00 and 18:30.

SIR HENRY MORGAN

Henry Morgan (1635–1688) is one of the Caribbean's wildest success stories. Born in **Wales**, he came to the Caribbean as a bondsman in the early 1650s. At the end of his contract, he joined the **buccaneers** of Jamaica, quickly becoming one of their leaders in the bloody plundering of Spanish ports throughout the Caribbean, culminating in the sack of **Panama**, the greatest city in the **Spanish Main**. He was knighted for his contribution to England's victories, and on the principle of 'set a thief to catch a thief' was made **Governor of Jamaica**, where he lived, prospered, and eventually died in 1688.

Above: *Tilted on its foundation by an earthquake in 1907, the Giddy House previously served as an artillery store.*

Fort Charles Maritime Museum **

After the earthquake of 1692, Port Royal was rebuilt and became the main Caribbean base of the **Royal Navy** for two centuries. The strongest of its defences was **Fort Charles**, established by Cromwell's troops when they occupied Jamaica in 1655 and strengthened in later years to become a formidable obstacle to would-be attackers. More than 100 massive cast-iron cannon bristle from the battlements of this solid red brick fortress, built to guard the approaches to the harbour from invasion by the French. In its heyday, these defences were augmented by a seawater moat, but the whitewashed garrison buildings and flagstoned parade square are much as they must have been in Nelson's time.

Within the walls is also the little **Maritime Museum**, which has a collection of finely detailed ship models and a miscellany of maritime memorabilia from the days of sail. Open 09:00–16:00 weekdays, 10:00–17:00 weekends.

Giddy House *

About 100 yards (91m) south of the fort, the small brick building half buried in the shingle of the nearby beach is known as the Giddy House, for obvious reasons. Tilted at a crazy angle, it was a victim not of the first Port Royal earthquake but of the 1907 earthquake, which clearly rocked it to its foundations. The plaque above the arched doorway reveals that it served as the **Royal Artillery Store**, built in 1888 during the reign of Queen Victoria. A large muzzle-loading cannon, tipped from its mounting on the massive brick emplacement next to the Giddy House, was another victim of the 1907 tremors, but beside it several more titanic 19th-century guns still point out to sea from the Victoria and Albert gun batteries.

NELSON'S QUARTERDECK

Among the commanders of **Fort Charles** was **Horatio Nelson**. He was only 20 when he was given command of the garrison in 1779, beginning the glorious career which was to lead to the birth of a legend. A plaque within the walls commemorates him, and the observation platform looking out to sea from the fortifications – where the young commander is said to have kept watch for the enemy's sails – is still known as Nelson's Quarterdeck, while the square in front of the fort is now named **Nelson Square**.

Archaeological and Historical Museum **

The small Archaeological and Historical Museum on Broad Street contains a collection of relics of old Port Royal, brought up from the sea bottom by fishermen's nets, dredged up by treasure seekers or discovered by scuba divers. Tales of pirate wealth keep people looking for fabled treasure swept into the sea by the earthquake three centuries ago. Though no great hoard of pieces of eight has ever been found, the museum has benefited from the continuing search, and boasts an interesting assortment of bits and pieces saved from the ocean bed. The museum occupies one of the rooms of the old **Naval Hospital,** a long building of cast iron construction which, though battered, has resisted several earthquakes. It was built in 1819 and overlooks Port Royal harbour. Open 09:00–16:00 weekdays, 10:00–17:00 weekends.

Old Gaol *

The Old Gaol on New Street is one of Port Royal's oldest buildings. It survived the 1692 earthquake and must have housed some notorious evil-doers in its time, but today it shows little signs of its grim past and houses a selection of souvenir and craft shops. Open 09:00–17:00 Monday–Saturday.

> **PIRATEERS**
>
> Many saw the destruction of **Port Royal** in 1692 as a judgement on the wicked ways of its inhabitants. Although its days as a pirate capital were curtailed, piracy continued and, despite the best efforts of the Royal Navy, pirates such as **Edward 'Blackbeard' Teach**, **Nicholas Brown** and **'Calico Jack' Rackham** continued to plague Jamaican waters well into the 18th century.

Below: *Over 100 giant cast-iron cannon line the battlements of historic Fort Charles.*

Above: *Morgan's Harbour Hotel is the base for excursions to cays off the Palisadoes Peninsula.*

Lime Cay ★★
As your plane made its descent into Norman Manley airport you may have spotted a scattering of a dozen coral cays lying offshore from Port Royal, in the open water south of the **Palisadoes Peninsula**. These miniature islands have brilliant white coral-sand beaches and warm shallow water, and are perfect havens for swimming, snorkelling and sunbathing. They can become rather busy at weekends, when they attract Kingstonians seeking a break from the city streets, but are much less crowded during the week. The **Morgan's Harbour Hotel**, overlooking the harbour a few hundred metres from the centre of Port Royal, operates boat trips to **Lime Cay**, the biggest of these islands and, on request, to its smaller neighbours.

ST ANDREW PARISH
The parish of St Andrew forms the hinterland of Kingston, with splendid scenery on the slopes of the **Blue Mountains** which, in turn, offer magnificent views of both Kingston and its picturesque coast. Only one proper road crosses the Blue Mountains – the B1, which runs from Kingston, via **Castleton**, to Buff Bay on the north coast. In the northeast of the parish there are a number of sights worth seeing on a day trip from the capital.

Castleton Botanical Gardens ★★
Gigantic tree ferns reminiscent of *Jurassic Park*, more than 30 different kinds of palm tree, azaleas and dozens of other brilliant tropical flowering plants are highlights of this delightful garden, 20 miles (32km) north of Kingston on route A3. Founded in 1862, Castleton boasts an enormous array of flora, with more than 1000 different types of flowers and plant. Open 07:00–18:00 daily.

FRUITS OF JAMAICA

Delicious **coconut** and **pineapple** are on every buffet table and you'll meet plenty of beach vendors happy to slice the top from a green drinking coconut with a few deft strokes. Less familiar fruit include the **star apple**, a green or purple fruit with sweet white pulp which is served with grapefruit or orange, and the **sweetsop**, a smaller, sweeter cousin of the **soursop** with green skin and sweet pulp.

Newcastle Fort *

The grounds of the **Jamaica Defence Force** training camp, 12 miles (19km) north of Kingston on route B1, were originally a British colonial garrison, and are now open to visitors. The crests of the Jamaican regiments – both past and present – adorn the walls of the parade ground and there are fine mountain views. Open 08:00–17:00 daily.

Hollywell Forest Park

Situated on the B1, some 3 miles (5km) north of Newcastle, the woodlands of Hollywell remain a delight for both birdwatchers and walkers, with extensive hilltop views of Kingston. Hollywell was hit hard by Hurricane Gilbert in 1988, but many new trees have been planted and its forests are well on the way to recovery. Open 09:00–17:00 daily.

Cinchona Botanical Gardens **

Cinchona, perched high on the **Grand Ridge** of the Blue Mountains, 22 miles (35km) northeast of Kingston, is a colourful estate of landscaped gardens planted with exotic flowering trees and shrubs. Its original purpose, when set up in 1868, was to grow cinchona, the tree from which the anti-malarial drug quinine is extracted, and Assam tea. Neither crop was successful, and Cinchona became an ornamental garden instead. Open daily.

HEALING HERBS

Jamaicans have always placed great faith in natural herbal cures for ailments and – especially in rural Jamaica, where modern health care is out of the reach of many – numerous herbal cures are still in use. **Coconut water** is said to be good for the kidneys, and **fever grass tea** is drunk to alleviate aches and fever. One traditional healing plant which has found favour worldwide as a cure-all for everything from sunburn to eczema is the **aloe**, used as an ingredient in sunburn lotions, shampoos, health drinks and skin toners.

Left: *Over 1000 different types of flowers and plants may be found at thriving Castleton Botanical Gardens north of Kingston, founded in 1862.*

BLUE MOUNTAINS

Peaking at altitudes of more than 7000ft (2200m) above sea level, the sierras of the **Blue Mountains** and the adjoining **John Crow Mountains** are visible from points all over the north, south and east coasts. Shrouded in mists the colour of cigar smoke, it's easy to see how the Blue Mountains got their name – though at close quarters their slopes are verdant and in many places cloaked in near-virgin forest. So far above the sea, the climate of the Blue Mountains is distinctly cooler than that of the coast, with more than 300 inches (7610mm) annual rainfall, and is ideal for growing coffee, bananas and another less reputable crop – ganja. The Grand Ridge of the Blue Mountains is almost 30 miles long and some 12 miles (20km) wide. Running diagonally across the island from northwest to southeast, merging at its eastern end with the John Crow range – which, in turn, runs parallel to the east coast of the island – the Grand Ridge is dominated by five summits: **John Crow**, at 5750ft (1762m); **Sir Johns**, at 6332ft (1930m); **Mossman's Peak**, at 6703ft (2043m); **High Peak**, at 6812ft (2076m); and **Blue Mountain Peak**, at 7402ft (2256m), the highest point in Jamaica. For the more energetic and adventurous, several tour companies organise trekking into the **Blue Mountains–John Crow National Park**, which occupies almost 200,000 acres (89,000ha) around the Blue Mountain Peak.

GANJA

Unless you look unbelievably straight, at some point during your stay you will be offered a taste of ganja (*cannabis indica*). **Rastafarians** regard it as a sacramental herb. Dope contributes millions to Jamaica's illicit economy. What you are offered will certainly be described as **'sensimilla'** – the strongest kind – but is more likely to be **'bush'** – the commonest and cheapest. Ganja is no more harmful than other drugs such as tobacco and alcohol, and in Jamaica even policemen have been known to light up. However, possession is illegal, with potentially heavy penalties, and dogs trained to detect it will sniff your luggage as you leave Jamaica and on arrival back in the US or UK.

Right: *Coffee cultivated in the verdant Blue Mountain range is generally exported for sale abroad, where it manages to command high prices in the frequently volatile inter-national coffee market.*

BLUE MOUNTAINS

Left: *The aptly named Blue Mountain Peak, seen from the north, is Jamaica's highest peak at 7402ft (2256m), with a climate that is distinctly cooler than on the coast.*

Blue Mountain Peak ★★★

The walk to the top of Blue Mountain Peak is rather a tough one, but the rewards along the way include the varied and colourful birdlife, flowers, plants and butterflies of the mountains – and some of the most magnificent views in Jamaica. Most treks start from **Mavis Bank**, a small settlement at the end of the road from Kingston via **Gordon Town** (about an hour's drive). The ascent takes at least four hours, so if you want to be on the peak in time for the magnificent sunrise you have to hit the trail by 02.00. The trail is steep and strenuous at the start, but the going gets a little easier as you climb higher. From the peak, the view is of tangled green jungle sloping down into blue mists, with the Caribbean sparkling in the distance beyond the **Kingston Plains** and the urban sprawl of the capital city far below. Any reasonably fit person should be able to complete the walk, which requires no technical skill, and if you can spare a couple of days from your sightseeing schedule it is very well worth doing.

RUM

Made from the treacly **molasses** extracted from sugar cane, rum in a dozen different guises has been Jamaica's favourite tipple since the days of the buccaneers. The most popular brands are **Wray**, **Sangster** and **Appleton**, all of which produce white rum – most often used in cocktails and punches – as well as gold rum aged in oak casks. Strongest of all is **overproof rum**. With an alcohol content of up to 80% – and a kick like a bucking bronco! – it should be drunk with extreme caution.

Kingston & St Andrew at a Glance

BEST TIMES TO VISIT
Jamaica's climate is moderate year-round, but the heat and humidity May–November, along with seasonal rains, make it officially off-season.

GETTING THERE
Norman Manley International Airport is on the Palisadoes Peninsula, 10 miles (16km) and 30 minutes from downtown Kingston. Touts offer rides into town, but most main hotels operate shuttles. Air Jamaica's **Air Jamaica Express** flies to Kingston from Montego Bay and Negril, arriving at **Tinson Pen Airport** 2 miles (3km) from the city.

GETTING AROUND
Car hire: Drivers must be over 21 and have British, EU, US or Canadian licence. Car hire is expensive; not recommended within Kingston. **Avis** (tel: 924 8013/926 1560); **Budget** (tel: 924 8762/8170, or 938 2189/2189. Four-wheel-drives essential for Blue Mountain trips.
Taxis: Kingston's best travel option, but agree on the fare before boarding. Licensed cabs have red **Public Passenger Vehicle** (PPV) licence plates.
Buses: Crowded and uncomfortable – and a real risk from pickpockets and bagsnatchers.
Tourist coaches: Jamaican Union of Travellers Associations (JUTA), tel: 926 1537, runs tourist taxis (comfortable but not cheap) and shuttles between resorts.

WHERE TO STAY
New Kingston Area
LUXURY
Wyndham Hotel Kingston, 77 Knutsford Boulevard, Kingston 5, tel: 926 5430-9, fax: 929 7439. The best: 489 balconied rooms with views; five restaurants and five bars. Popular.
Le Meridien Jamaica Pegasus, 81 Knutsford Boulevard, Kingston 5, tel: 926 3690, fax: 929 5855. Four-star hotel in financial district, now under management of international chain. Tennis court, pool, restaurants, bars, nightly entertainment and facilities for handicapped travellers.
Crowne Plaza Hotel, 211a Constant Spring Road, Manor Park, Kingston 8, tel: 925 7674, fax: 925 5757. New international hotel with 133 rooms, two restaurants, pool, tennis, nightly entertainment.

MID-RANGE
Sutton Place Hotel, 11 Ruthven Road, Kingston 10, tel: 926 1207, fax: 926 8443. 180 rooms with air-con; pool.
Terra Nova Hotel, 17 Waterloo Road, Kingston 10, tel: 926 2211, fax: 929 9334. Secluded, elegant; 21 rooms. Own pool, restaurants, bar.
Mayfair Hotel, PO Box 163, Kingston 10, tel: 926 6160, fax: 929 7441. Eight villas with garden. Pool, restaurant, bar.
Medallion Hall Hotel, 53 Hope Road, Kingston 6, tel/fax: 927 5721, 21 rooms above King's House.

BUDGET
Altamont Court Hotel, 1–3 Altamont Terrace, Kingston 5, tel: 929 4497, fax: 929 2118. Central, family owned; pool.
Courtleigh Hotel, 31 Trafalgar Road, Kingston 10, tel: 929 9000, fax: 926 7744. 37 rooms, two suites, pool and its disco.

Port Royal Area
LUXURY
Morgan's Harbour Hotel, Port Royal, tel: 967 8030, fax: 967 8073. Near city, seafront restaurant, marina, watersports.

Blue Mountains
LUXURY
Strawberry Hill, Irish Town, tel: 944 8400, fax: 944 8408. Remote, self-contained; 12 villas halfway up Blue Mountains. Airy rooms. Airport shuttle and helicopter available for fee.

WHERE TO EAT
Kingston has a choice of eating places, from roadside shacks to hotel restaurants, but none reach gourmet status. On a budget, head for a 'jerk centre'.

Central Kingston
LUXURY
Le Pavilion, Jamaica Pegasus Hotel, 81 Knutsford Boulevard, tel: 926 2690. Expensive hotel restaurant with international menu attracting power elite.
Isabella's, Crowne Plaza Hotel, 211a Constant Spring Road, Kingston 8, tel: 925 7674, fax: 925 5757. Gourmet restaurant in Kingston's newest hotel.

Kingston & St Andrew at a Glance

Devonshire Restaurant, Devon House, 26 Hope Road, tel: 929 7046. Surf-and-turf and international dishes.
Blue Mountain Inn, Gordon Town, tel: 927 1700. Historic inn in Blue Mountain foothills.

MID-RANGE
Hot Pot, 2 Altamont Terrace, Kingston 5, tel: 929 3906. Traditional dishes such as curry goat, 'run down', jerk pork.
The Fish Place, Constant Spring Road, Kingston 10, tel: 924 4063. Excellent fish, lobster and seafood in fashionable part of town.
Guilt Trip, 20 Barbican Road, Kingston 6, tel: 977 5130. Sinfully delicious Caribbean gourmet cooking.
Heather's, 9 Haining Road, Kingston 5, tel: 960 7739 Imaginative blend of Jamaican and Middle Eastern influences.
Red Bones, 21 Braemar Ave, Kingston 10, tel: 978 8262. Caribbean gourmet cooking and venue for live blues music.

BUDGET
Queen of Sheba, 56 Hope Rd, Kingston 6, tel: 978 0510. Ethiopian restaurant for tasty, mainly vegetarian rasta dishes.
Jade Gardens, Shop 54, Sovereign Centre, Kingston 6, tel: 978 3476. Affordable Chinese Restaurant.
Lychee Gardens, Shop 34, New Kingston Shopping Centre, Kingston 5, tel: 929 8619. Conveniently located and affordable.

Port Royal
LUXURY
Sir Henry's, Morgan's Harbour Hotel, Port Royal, tel: 924 8464. Best view of harbour; fresh seafood.

SHOPPING

From modern complexes (luxury and imported goods) to craft markets (paintings, beachwear, woodcarvings and baskets). US cruise passengers provide most of the clientele, and prices and products are made to appeal to them. Jamaica claims 20–40% less on duty-free prices than rival Caribbean destinations.

TOURS AND EXCURSIONS

Touring Society of Jamaica, tel: 954 2383. Variety of sightseeing and birding tours in and around Kingston and Jamaica.
Kingston Highlights Tours, tel: 929 5078. Half day tour of the sights of Kingston, including Bob Marley Museum, Cultural Training Centre, University of West Indies.
Kingston and Port Royal Tours, tel: 929 5078, Highlights of Kingston and Port Royal including Nelson's quarterdeck and the Port Royal Archaeological Museum.

Blue Mountain RidgeTour, tel: 929 5078. Day tour of the national park, with Blue Mountain coffee tasting.
Greenlight Tours, 19 Carlton Crescent, Kingston 10, tel: 929 9190. Tours of Kingston and Port Royal; excursions to Ocho Rios and Port Antonio.
Blue Mountain Peak Hike, Whitfield Hall, Mavis Bank, St Thomas, tel: 927 0986. Meals and accommodation at park, and guides for the ascent.

USEFUL CONTACTS

Jamaica Tourist Board (HO), ICWI Building, 2 St Lucia Ave, Kingston 5, tel: 929 9200
Jamaica Hotel and Tourist Association, 2 Ardenne Road, Kingston 10, tel: 926 3635, fax: 929 1054.
Jamaica Union of Travellers Association, Kingston Chapter, 85 Knutsford Boulevard, Kingston 5, tel: 926 1537.
Stuart's Travel Service, 9 Cecelio Avenue, Kingston 10, tel: 926 4291. An American Express Travel Service office for cheque refunds, card replacement, tours, tickets, reconfirmation and other card-member services.

KINGSTON	J	F	M	A	M	J	J	A	S	O	N	D
AVERAGE TEMP. °C	30	30	30	32	32	33	33	33	33	32	32	32
AVERAGE TEMP. °F	86	86	86	90	90	92	92	92	92	90	90	90
HOURS OF SUN DAILY	10	10	10	9	9	6	6	6	6	4	4	9
RAINFALL mm	25	25	25	75	100	75	50	100	150	175	150	25
RAINFALL ins.	1	1	1	3	4	3	2	4	6	7	6	1
DAYS OF RAINFALL	1	1	1	6	7	6	5	10	12	14	12	1

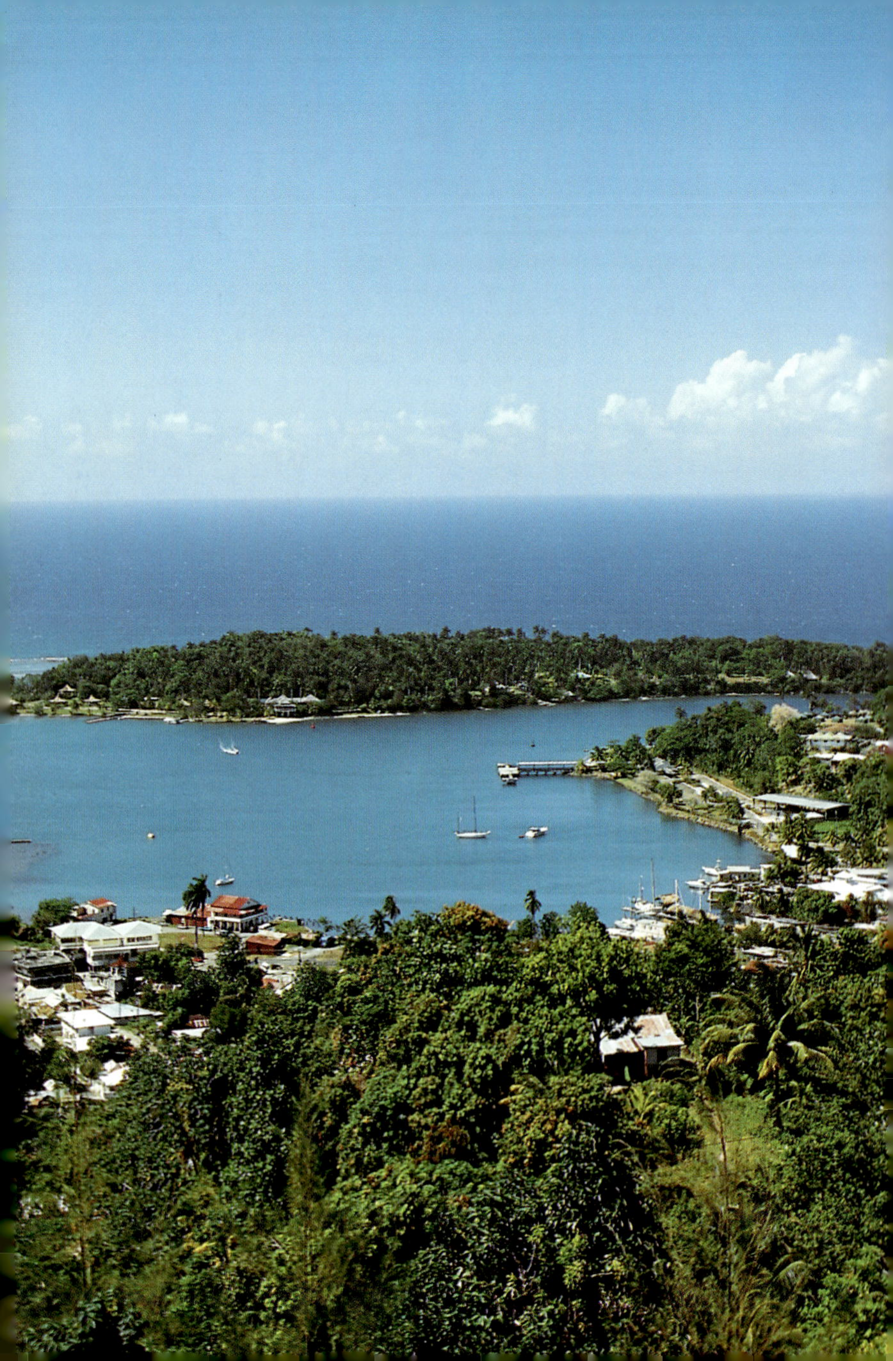

3
Portland and St Thomas

Rugged mountainscapes, thick tropical rainforests, coffee plantations, sea cliffs and the exclusive hideaways of the rich and famous are some of the characteristics of Jamaica's two easternmost parishes. Together with St Andrew (the parish surrounding Kingston), **Portland** and **St Thomas** make up the county of **Surrey**. The latter two parishes are divided by the **Grand Ridge** of the Blue Mountains. To the east, beyond the Blue Mountain range, the **John Crow Mountains** rise steeply, cutting the Portland hinterland off from the sea. Like the Cockpit Country of Trelawny parish in the northwest of the island, the hill country of Portland and St Thomas is one of the most inaccessible and sparsely inhabited parts of the island, and there are no main roads through the heart of this territory. In centuries long past, its dripping virgin forest and thick undergrowth provided a refuge for fierce – and fearless – bands of proud Maroon warriors, whose descendants still dwell in remote mountain villages.

The coasts of Portland and St Thomas, in contrast with the region's rugged interior, hide some of Jamaica's most exclusive, elegant and sophisticated resorts. On the north coast lies Port Antonio, the birthplace of tourism in Jamaica and still a favoured retreat. From here back-to-nature sightseeing excursions run into the interior, exploring the region's caves, waterfalls and deep jungle gorges, or experiencing the excitement of river rafting.

DON'T MISS

*** **Port Antonio:** beautiful scenery, islands and fine beaches.
*** **Blue Hole:** spectacular lagoon of vivid turquoise water.
*** **Rio Grande:** bamboo rafting through stands of giant bamboo.
*** **Blue Mountain Peak:** fantastic views from the highest summit in Jamaica.
** **Reach Falls:** beautiful series of cascades, one of the island's most striking sights.

Opposite: *Port Antonio's coastline is home to exclusive villas and resorts.*

50 PORTLAND AND ST THOMAS

Above: *The thrilling International Blue Marlin Tournament takes place off the shores of Port Antonio each October.*

Port Antonio

Turquoise waters dotted with small jungle-like islands, clear winding rivers, green hillsides, and beaches dotted with colourful fishing pirogues... the stunning beauty of the Port Antonio area has lured the bold and the beautiful since Errol Flynn's day and before. It is hard to believe today, looking at its quintessentially sleepy quaysides and streets, that this was where Jamaican tourism was born. Built around a natural harbour, the resorts and villas around this little port, some 70 miles (130km) northeast of Kingston, are among Jamaica's most exclusive and expensive. They still attract a clientele of Hollywood stars and minor Eurotrash, and the surrounding area has been a favourite location for movie producers since the 1960s. With the silhouetted peaks of the Blue Mountains as a backdrop, this is undoubtedly one of the island's most unspoilt resort areas, though the town itself has seen better days and has little in the way of sightseeing attractions.

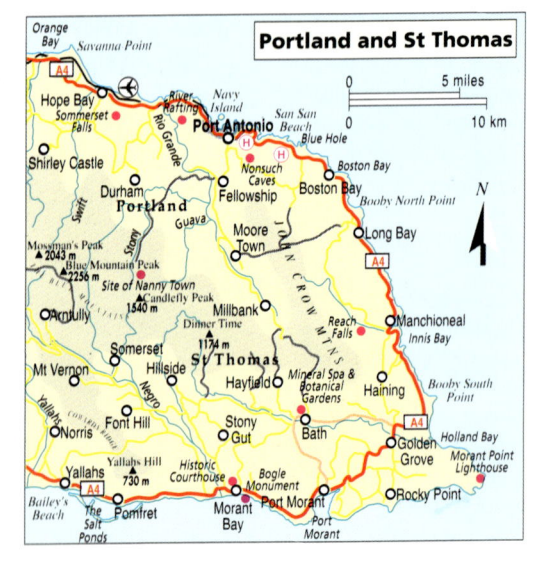

As its name implies, Port Antonio was named by the first Spanish settlers, who could hardly ignore such a haven, and they dubbed it Puerto Anton. But the hinterland was rugged and extremely ill-suited to cultivation, and other, more easily settled parts of the island attracted the attention of the Spaniards and their British successors. The first proper settlement at Port Antonio was in the early 18th century, but it remained a backwater fishing harbour until the late 19th century, when the advent of refrigerated cargo vessels brought about a Caribbean banana boom. The hillsides inland proved ideal for banana planting, and Port Antonio entered a golden age of prosperity. Banana shippers had the bright idea of bringing visitors to Jamaica from US ports to escape the chilly northern winter, and the first wealthy tourists set the tone for generations to come.

Fort George *

Port Antonio consists of two bays, **West Harbour** and **East Harbour**, which are divided by the **Titchfield Peninsula**. Titchfield School, at the tip of this peninsula, occupies the site of **Fort George**, which was built in 1729 to defend the harbours. A handful of cannon can be seen in the school grounds, surrounded by the 10ft (3m) thick walls of the original fort.

> **ERROL FLYNN**
>
> Appropriately for an actor who rose to Hollywood fame playing buccaneers like the legendary **Captain Blood** in movies set on the Spanish Main, Errol Flynn landed in Jamaica when in 1947 his yacht was blown off course in a storm and fell in love with the island immediately, buying **Navy Island**, off Port Antonio, and making his home there for the last decade of his life. Older residents still remember the glamour he and his film-star guests brought to **Port Antonio**, and he is also credited with launching river rafting on the **Rio Grande**.

Navy Island ***

Australian-born film star **Errol Flynn** put Navy Island on the map quite by chance – his yacht was forced to take shelter in Port Antonio harbour during a hurricane and he liked the place so much that he bought this small island just off Titchfield Point to use as his private hideaway. The island has two beaches, a hotel and a yacht club. Ferries and water taxis connect it with West Harbour 24 hours a day; the trip takes five minutes. Open 07:00–22:00 daily.

Below: *Beautiful Navy Island is open to visitors, accessible by water taxi.*

> **BLUE HOLES**
>
> Most of Jamaica's geology is **limestone**, and millennia of tropical rains have carved out extensive **cave systems** in the Jamaican hills, many of them still to be explored. The limestone rock has also been hollowed out by rain and wave action into deep water-filled 'blue holes' connecting to the sea, some of which offer exciting cave-diving adventures, such as **God's Well**, a 160ft (50m) sinkhole on the **Long Bay** coast.

Opposite: *Rafting on the Rio Grande is a popular activity and attracts company on the river.*
Below: *The Blue Hole is surprisingly deep, its water a remarkable shade of turquoise.*

Athenry Gardens and Nonsuch Caves **

About 2 miles (5km) southeast of Port Antonio, and 1000ft (330m) above sea level, this former coconut plantation embraces 185 acres (34ha) of rainforest and a profusion of spectacular tropical plants. The plantation affords fine views of the coast and the John Crow Mountains.

About a mile from Athenry, though still within the plantation grounds, are nine inter-connected caves, known as the **Nonsuch Caves**. The caves contain strange limestone and volcanic formations, as well as fossils, and are the haunt of hundreds of tiny bats. Open 09:00–16:00.

San San Beach ***

Port Antonio's best beach – the one that attracts the stars – is 5 miles (8km) east of town at San San, where a dazzling crescent of powdery coral sand is backed by three luxury hotels and a nine-hole golf course. The beach is private, and there is an entry charge for those not lucky enough to be staying at one of the luxury resorts there. Open 10:00–22:00 daily.

Blue Hole (Blue Lagoon) ***

A few hundred metres east of San San Beach, the Blue Hole, also called the **Blue Lagoon**, is at least 200ft (60m) deep – underwater explorer Jacques Cousteau is said to have dived to at least that depth and found no bottom. The 'hole' is a limestone sink and its almost luminous turquoise waters are ringed by vivid green foliage. It has been used as a location for many movies including the 1980 Brooke Shields teen film *Blue Lagoon*. Floodlit at night, the lagoon is a sight more memorable than any of the films which have been shot there, and you can only envy those who can afford the luxury of a private villa on its shores. Open 10:00–22:00 daily.

WEST OF PORT ANTONIO
Rio Grande ★★★

The bamboo rafts which are now used to carry tourists down Jamaica's longest river, were originally used by banana planters to ferry their crop to the coast at St Margaret's Bay, about 5 miles (8km) west of Port Antonio. Once again, it was the actor Errol Flynn who turned the Rio Grande into a vacation experience, taking guests staying at his Navy Island home on trips down the river. Today, the raft ride – on long, slender bamboo craft poled by singing gondoliers – takes about three hours and the route extends through lush jungle scenery. Visitors are able to take a raft trip day or night – it is especially popular on romantic moonlit nights. Rio Grande rafting is, however, one of Jamaica's most highly commercialised holiday activities, and it can seem that virtually every foot of the river bank has been staked out by somebody who is trying to sell you something. Open 09:00–15:30 daily.

Sommerset Falls ★

At Sommerset Falls, 12 miles (20km) west of Port Antonio, the **Daniels River** forms a series of pools and cataracts beneath a canopy of bamboos, ferns and wild bananas. Although the falls themselves are actually quite tame, visitors may choose to swim in a nearby chasm. Open 09:00–17:00.

SALTFISH AND ACKEE

It's hard to believe that something which so closely resembles scrambled egg grows on a tree, but **ackee**, the favourite Jamaican breakfast dish, comes from the pod-like fruits of a tree imported to the island from West Africa. Ackee is usually served with **salt cod**, originally imported from Newfoundland as a cheap food for slaves and now regarded as a luxury to be eaten on special occasions. You will find saltfish and ackee on most resort breakfast buffets.

MOORE TOWN

Moore Town, a clutch of simple wooden homes and buildings only 10 miles (16km) south of Port Antonio, is a step back on the road to ancestral Africa. It is the capital of the proud **Windward Maroons**, one of two communities created in the 18th and 19th centuries by escapees from slavery. Moore Town and the region around it, under a treaty signed between the British and the Maroons in 1739, have some degree of self-government, with day-to-day affairs administered by a Maroon council of 24 headed by a hereditary 'Colonel'. Other Maroon communities in the neighbourhood include **Comfort Castle**, **Seaman's Valley** and **Ginger Town**, but the Maroon remain proudly aloof from tourism and to make the most of a trip to their mountains it is advisable to contact the Maroon Council, through the Jamaica Tourist Board, in order to arrange a guided visit.

Sam Sharpe Museum *

The small Sam Sharpe Museum located on Main Street commemorates one of Jamaica's national heroes, the rebel leader Sam Sharpe, who inspired the **Christmas Rebellion** of 1831–2 which was to lead to the ending of the slave system in 1834. The museum also tells of the Maroons' unique dialect and way of life, which retain strong West African elements. Open 09:00–17:00 Monday–Friday.

Bump Grave *

Outside Moore Town's small school, situated just off Main Street, stands a plain stone column which is said to mark the final resting place of **Nanny**, the 17th-century chieftainess who governed over the Windward Maroons. The much-revered Nanny was declared a national heroine in 1975, when the monument was placed here. The site of Nanny Town, her capital, is said to be in the Blue Mountains high above Moore Town, but it was completely destroyed in 1734 and no trace remains.

MAROONS

Descended from runaway **Spanish slaves** and **Coromantee warriors** from the **Gold Coast** (now Ghana) who escaped in the **Clarendon** slave uprising of 1690, the Maroons are aptly named (from *cimarron*, Spanish for 'wild'). Their bush warfare and survival skills helped them maintain their freedom, and even after two wars against the British – the second ending in the deportation of 600 of them to Canada – they managed to keep control of their own affairs, under their own rulers, though they had to agree to return runaway slaves to white custody. Today, the Maroons are concentrated around **Moore Town**, in the mountains south of Port Antonio, and **Maroon Town**, in the Cockpit Country.

EAST COAST
Long Bay *

Around 12 miles (20km) east of Port Antonio, Long Bay has two of Jamaica's most spectacular beaches. You may at first be surprised at the lack of tourism development here, since the location seems ideal, but the exposed crescent bays are vulnerable to high seas in the hurricane season – and even in calmer weather there is a fierce undertow – which makes swimming dangerous and has deterred even daring fishermen from settling here.

Manchioneal *

Manchioneal is the only good anchorage on this exposed coast, and a small fishing hamlet has grown up around its natural harbour. The deep blue bay and the colourful wooden dugout canoes hauled up on Manchioneal's narrow beach make it a perfect photo opportunity, but there is little to see or do other than to relax and take in the sunshine and the majestic setting.

Reach Falls **

Reach Falls, about 20 miles (32km) southeast of Port Antonio, is one of the island's most spectacular sights, rivalling the more famous Dunn's River Falls near Ocho Rios. The falls cascade in four cataracts, the tallest of which is some 40ft (13m) high, and each terminates in a deep green pool (although swimming is allowed, strong undercurrents make it rather dangerous). A gaggle of dreadlocked higglers sell the usual array of carvings and ornaments. Open daily, daylight hours.

BANANAS

Bananas became big business in **Port Antonio** in the 1870s, when thousands of tons were exported to the US and Britain. Plenty of bananas are still grown in Jamaica, but the fruit is no longer a top export crop. If you are used to the standardised yellow variety sold in your local supermarket, you'll be astonished by the different varieties piled high in Jamaican markets, from small red fruit no longer than your finger to giant green plantain, a savoury cousin of the banana which is served fried.

Below: *Long Bay's exposed position has deterred development.*

BATH

Rather aptly named after the renowned English spa, Bath has been favoured for its natural hot springs ever since 1699. This small town is clearly long past its Victorian heyday, when it attracted the very wealthiest of trend-setters on the island to bathe in its supposedly healing waters, but visitors are still welcome to emulate the early holidaymakers, and unwind in the soothing waters of this picturesque district.

Above: River waters near Bath are said to have medicinal properties.

> **FOREST FLAME**
>
> Jamaica wouldn't be the same without the blazing scarlet, orange and vermilion flowers of the 'Flame of the Forest' or **poinciana**. Native to Madagascar, its spreading boughs shade many island roads and homes. The **flame tree** flowers for much of the year, but between February and April its flowers and foliage give way to bare branches and gigantic seed pods. Up to 20 inches (50cm) long, these make natural rattles for children and maracas for reggae and calypso musicians.

Bath Fountain Hotel *

The Bath Fountain Hotel is 2 miles (3km) north of town and its real attraction is its natural hot spring baths, which are open to visitors and are held to cure all manner of ills. A half-hour wallow will certainly ease muscular aches and pains. The waters of the mineral springs have high concentrations of sulphur and calcium, and emerge from a source close to the rather aptly-named **Sulphur River** at temperatures of 50–55°C (115–128°F). Open daily.

Botanical Gardens *

When not steaming themselves in the thermal baths, Victorian visitors strolled in the botanical gardens, founded in 1779 to cultivate exotic plants imported to Jamaica by seafarers such as **Captain William Bligh** of HMS *Bounty*, who brought the breadfruit to the island. The colourful gardens, adjoining the small church in the centre of Bath, are very photogenic and still worth a short visit. Open daily.

St Thomas Coast
Morant Point Lighthouse *

The red-and-white striped lighthouse which marks Jamaica's southeastern extremity seems to lean at a precarious angle, like the Leaning Tower of Pisa, and looks set to eventually topple into the Caribbean. The cast-iron tower was made in London and the prefabricated segments bolted together and erected at Morant Point in 1841. If the keeper is in, you may be able to persuade him to take you to the open gallery at the top, from which there are panoramic views of the coast and out to sea. The lighthouse is open to visitors at varying times, and only in daylight hours.

Port Morant *

Like Port Antonio, Port Morant – a fine natural harbour on the St Thomas south coast, some 50 miles (80km) east of Kingston – flourished when the banana industry took off but later lost some of it lustre. However, unlike Port Antonio it has never attracted flocks of rich northern holidaymakers. Port Morant bay has small beaches at **Lyssons**, on the west side, and **Roselle**, on the east, which are popular with local people at weekends.

Morant Bay *

Morant Bay, now a quiet town on the south coast where the road from Bath meets the round-the-island highway, some 40 miles (64km) east of Kingston, was the scene of bloody confrontation between Jamaica's white ruling class and emancipated, but still oppressed, black Jamaicans. The **Morant Bay Rebellion** of 1865, led by preacher **Paul Bogle**, left 28 dead. In reprisal, the authorities hanged Bogle, legislator **George William Gordon**, and 430 accused rebels. Thousands more were savagely flogged. But this barbaric response backfired on

> **RARE PARROTS**
>
> Two of Jamaica's parrot species are found nowhere else in the world and are considered endangered – due largely to the destruction of their habitat and the poaching of eggs and fledglings for the pet trade. The **yellow-billed parrot** (*Amazona collaria*) is one of Jamaica's loveliest birds, around 11 inches (28cm) in size with primrose-yellow beak, rose-pink throat and green back and wings, with turquoise highlights on the head, tail and wings. The even rarer **black-billed parrot** (*Amazona agilis*) is 10 inches (25cm) in size, with charcoal-grey beak and eyes and green plumage.

Below: *Exotic plants such as this ginger lily fare well in Jamaica's climate.*

THE MONGOOSE

The mongoose was introduced from **India** to deal with cane rats and snakes infesting sugar cane. Jamaica is now almost snake-free – with its surviving serpents now endangered. The mongoose has also wiped out several native bird species and continues to endanger others, including poultry, making it a far greater pest than the snakes ever were.

the plantocracy, and an investigation into the affair by a British Royal Commission led to the island being declared a Crown Colony, with the planters losing much of their power to oppress black Jamaicans.

The unusually powerful **Paul Bogle Monument**, a memorial to the leader of the uprising, sculpted by Edna Manley, stands in Morant Bay's town square. Nearby is **Morant Bay Fort**, which was built in 1773. The fort encloses a park commemorating those executed after the 1865 violence, and 79 skeletons found interred behind the walls of the fort during digging in 1965 were buried here in a common grave. Old iron cannon, dating from the 19th century, still stand on the battlements.

Yallahs

Midway between Morant Bay and Kingston, on the A4 coastal highway, Yallahs is little more than a truck-stop, surrounded by countryside which is almost desert-like by Jamaican standards, as it lies in the rain-shadow of the Blue Mountains. Yallahs has two minor attractions for those with a special interest in history or ornithology.

Below: *Morant Bay is a peaceful town on the south coast, no longer touched by the events of its somewhat turbulent past.*

ST THOMAS COAST

Left: *Hanged for his part in the Morant Bay rebellion that was violently crushed in 1865, Paul Bogle is now held as a national hero.*

Yallah Ponds *

On the coast a few hundred metres east of Yallahs village begins a narrow natural breakwater, formed by silt deposited by the broad, shallow **Yallahs River**. This stretches for almost 5 miles (8km) and encloses a vast, shallow brine lagoon which is a haven for flocks of seabirds that feed on the huge shoals of brine shrimp and other plankton breeding in the salty water.

Kach Mansong Monument *

Kach Mansong, also called **Three Fingered Jack**, was an escaped slave who took to a life of banditry in the foothills of the Blue Mountains in the late 18th century. Regarded as a murderer by the British authorities, he was a Robin Hood figure to many enslaved Jamaicans and is commemorated by a monument erected by the Jamaican National Heritage Trust. The site of the monument, beside the road 6 miles (10km) west of Yallahs on the A4, is the spot where he was ambushed and killed in 1781 by Maroon trackers in the pay of the authorities.

THE FLAG

Jamaica's black, green and yellow national flag, run up for the first time on 6 August 1962, was inspired by both **Norman Manley**, leader of the People's National Party and one of the fathers of Jamaican independence, and by his great rival, **Alexander Bustamante**, the country's first prime minister. Proudly pro-British, Bustamante wanted a flag reminiscent of the Union Flag of Britain, while Manley believed the new banner should symbolise all the peoples of Jamaica. The result is a black, green and gold national flag incorporating a **St Andrew's Cross**. Its colours fly over official buildings and adorn Rasta hats and countless holiday T-shirts.

Portland & St Thomas at a Glance

BEST TIMES TO VISIT

Jamaica's climate is moderate year-round, but the heat and humidity May–November, along with seasonal rains, make it officially off-season.

GETTING THERE

By Air: Air Jamaica Express has daily flights to Port Antonio from both Kingston (about 20 mins) and Montego Bay (about 45 mins).

By Land: If you are travelling on a package tour, your tour company will provide minibus transfer from Kingston, the nearest airport, or from Ocho Rios. Public transport is thin on the ground, and the only realistic alternatives to organised tours are self-drive **cars** or **taxis**. Port Antonio is approximately 60 miles (100km) northeast of Kingston, and the steep, winding drive through the Blue Mountains takes three hours or more.

GETTING AROUND

The only feasible way of travelling within Portland and St Thomas is by **taxi** or **hire car**: **Eastern Rent a Car**, 23 Harbour Street, Port Antonio, tel: 993 3624. **Buses** are too infrequent and irregular to be useful to the visitor. A coastal highway, the A4, runs all the way from the Portland/St Mary parish line in the north, through Port Antonio, Manchioneal, Morant Bay and Yallahs on the south coast to Kingston. The B1, a remarkable piece of road-building with many hairpin bends, cuts north through the Blue Mountains from Kingston to Buff Bay on the north coast, where it meets the A4. During the July–September rainy season, many of the unsurfaced roads in the region may become virtually impassable.

WHERE TO STAY

Almost all of the accommodation in the Port Antonio area is at the luxury end of the range and is priced accordingly. However, there is virtually no accommodation available beyond the Port Antonio area.

LUXURY

Dragon Bay, Zion Hill, Port Antonio, tel: 993 3281, fax: 993 3284. Luxury villas on 54 acres (22ha) of grounds. Each of the private villas has one suite and two bedrooms. Spectacular beach and snorkelling in private bay, tennis courts and even a jogging track.

Navy Island Marina Resort, Navy Island, Port Antonio, tel: 993 2667, fax: 929 1123. Luxury hotel, 13 rooms on Navy Island, with its own marina, beaches, tennis and volleyball courts, pool and restaurants; nature trails through 64 acres (26ha).

Trident Villas & Hotel, PO Box 119, Anchovy, Port Antonio, tel: 993 2602, fax: 993 2590. Luxury establishment, with 26 bedrooms furnished with colonial antiques, private balconies and verandas. Private beach, pool, tennis courts, restaurant and two bars.

Jamaica Palace Hotel, PO Box 277, Williamsfield, Port Antonio, tel: 993 2020, fax: 993 3459. Luxury hotel on the beach.

Goblin Hill Villas (San San), 11 East Avenue, Kingston 10, tel: 925 8108, fax: 925 6248. Lush 12-acre (5ha) retreat on the exclusive San San Estate; 28 villas with breathtaking beach views.

MID-RANGE

Bonnie View Plantation Hotel, PO Box 82, Richmond Hill, Port Antonio, tel: 993 2752, fax: 993 2862. Small, charming hotel, 22 rooms on 25-acre (10ha) working plantation. Fine views of the sea and the mountains. Good base for riding and hiking excursions.

Hotel Mocking Bird Hill, PO Box 254, Port Antonio, tel: 993 7267, fax: 993 7133. 10 rooms, restaurant and bar five minutes' walk from beach.

Fern Hill Club Hotel & Villa Resort, Mile Gully Road, PO Box 100, Port Antonio, tel: 993 3222, fax: 993 2257.

Portland & St Thomas at a Glance

All-inclusive, with 40 double-/twin rooms, 16 with whirlpool spa; nightly entertainment, restaurant, two bars. Located on San San Beach.

Where to Eat

Port Antonio
Luxury
Admiralty Club, Navy Island Resort and Marina, Navy Island. Splendid seafood and international dishes in Port Antonio's most romantic setting.
Blue Lagoon Restaurant, Blue Lagoon, tel: 993 8491. Magnificent location overlooking the splendid lagoon, which is floodlit at night. Fine dining and a good range of cocktails.

Mid-range
Bonnie View Plantation Hotel PO Box 82, Richmond Hill, Port Antonio. Worth visiting as much for the marvellous view from the terrace as for the Caribbean and international menu.
DeMontevin Lodge, Titchfield Street, Port Antonio, tel: 993 2604. Jamaican cuisine in a delightfully restored 18th-century building, once the home of an English admiral.

Budget
Boston Beach Jerk Centre, Boston Bay (no tel). About 8 miles (12km) east of Port Antonio, well worth visiting (as Jamaicans do) for probably the best jerk pork, chicken and fish in Jamaica, sold from a line of small beachside stalls, each with its own speciality on the menu. Look out for piquant boiled shrimp and junga, a locally caught freshwater crayfish. The best time to visit is during the day.

Shopping

Unlike Kingston, Ocho Rios, and Montego Bay (all of which have extensive shopping facilities catering to the American cruise passengers who tend to pass through), Port Antonio has very few worthwhile retail outlets and no big shopping malls.
Freeport Giftland, City Centre Plaza, Port Antonio, is a small complex of duty-free shops where Jamaican rum and cigars are the most attractive purchases on offer.
Designer's Gallery, Jamaica Palace Hotel, sells Jamaican carvings, paintings and beach clothing, all of which tend to be highly priced.

Tours and Excursions

Day on Navy Island, tel/fax: 993 2667. A 7-minute boat ride from the mainland, guided tour of the 64-acre (26ha) resort and former home of Errol Flynn, watersports. The island is open to non-residents; 24hr ferry.
Crystal Springs, Buff Bay, tel: 993 2609. Orchids and tropical birds to be seen on guided tour of former sugar-cane plantation, now a 156-acre (63ha) ecotourism attraction with picnic ground and botanical garden.
Rio Grande Rafting, Rafter's Rest, St Margaret's Bay, tel: 993 2778. An 8 mile (13km) guided raft trip takes between two and four hours.
Riding: Bonnie View Plantation Hotel, PO Box 82, Richmond Hill, Port Antonio, tel: 993 2752, fax: 448 5398. Organises guided horse-riding and hiking in the foothills inland from Port Antonio.
Blue Mountain Bicycle Ride, Port Antonio, tel: 974 7075. Ride a mountain bike down Blue Mountain roads and trails with an experienced guide.

Useful Contacts

Jamaica Tourist Board, City Centre Plaza, PO Box 151, Port Antonio, tel: 993 3051, fax: 993 2117.
Jamaica Union of Travellers Association, Port Antonio Chapter, 17 Harbour Street, Port Antonio, tel: 993 2684. Taxis, airport and resort transfers, and tours to all the popular sightseeing attractions of the region.

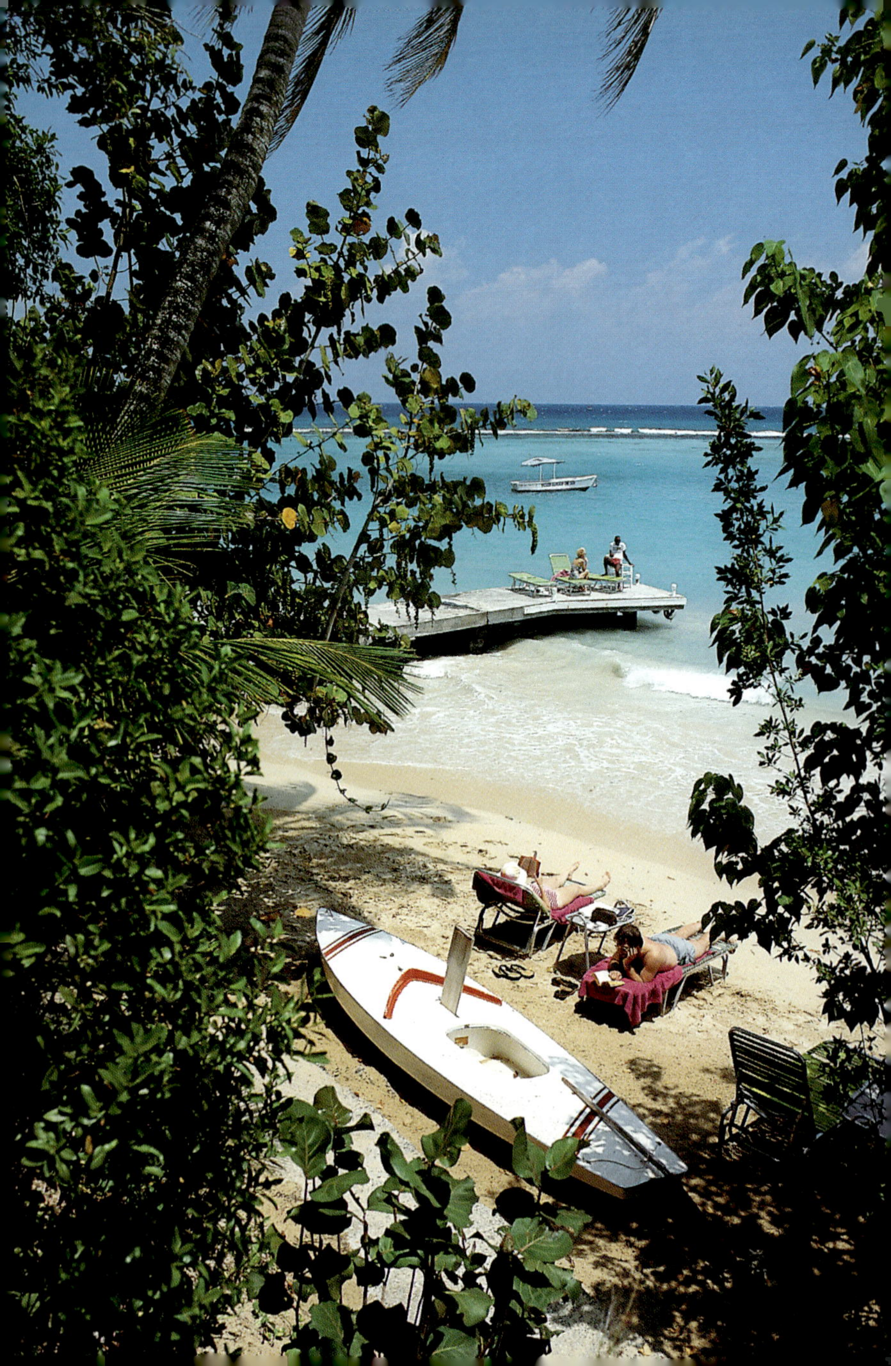

4
St Ann and St Mary

The parishes of St Ann and St Mary occupy the central third of Jamaica's north coast and its hinterland, with some splendid beaches and natural harbours backed by a coastal plain of sugar-cane fields rising gradually to rolling hills. The scenery here is pastoral rather than grand, with hills rising to only 2759ft (800m) at their highest point.

St Ann Parish can claim, in a sense, to be the heart of modern Jamaican history, for it was on this coast, where the appropriately named village of **Discovery Bay** now stands, that Christopher Columbus made his first landfall on the island, naming the spot **Rio Bueno**. The ruined foundations of **Sevilla la Nueva**, the first settlement founded by his conquistadors, may still be seen at **St Ann's Bay**, but the Spaniards soon moved their headquarters to **Villa de la Vega** (now Spanish Town) on the south coast, which had a much better anchorage. It was later from St Ann Parish that the last Spaniards fled Jamaica – from the shores of **Runaway Bay**, now a popular north coast resort – after being defeated by the British in 1658.

After the Spaniards came the British sugar planters, who left the fertile coastal plains patchworked with cane plantations. As sugar declined in importance, the north coast became a thriving centre for a new Jamaican boom industry – **tourism**. Among the first sun-seeking migrants to north shore resorts were wealthy expatriates such as English actor, playwright and musician Sir Noel Coward, and James Bond creator Ian Fleming, both of whom had villas overlooking the sea. In their steps have

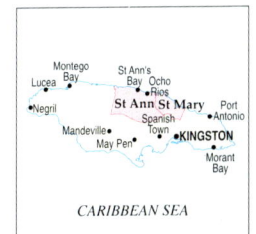

CARIBBEAN SEA

DON'T MISS

*** **Ocho Rios:** some of Jamaica's finest beaches and resorts.
*** **Dunn's River Falls:** the island's most famous waterfalls.
*** **Green Grotto:** explore deep limestone caverns on foot or by boat.
*** **Firefly:** Sir Noel Coward's lovely villa, with magnificent views.
** **White River:** rafting experience through tropical riverside scenery.
** **Harmony Hall:** fine wooden traditional residence with excellent art collection.

Opposite: *A succession of superb beaches lines the north coast of Jamaica.*

ADMIRAL NELSON

Horatio Nelson (1758–1805) joined the Royal Navy in 1770, spending much of the early part of his naval career in Jamaica and the Caribbean, where he was promoted to commander in 1778, returning in 1782–3 and again in 1784–87. Nelson is as well known for his defiance of orders, and physical disabilities – an eye lost at Calvi in 1794, and a right arm at Santa Cruz three years later – as for his victories in the French wars. He was made vice-admiral and created **Viscount Nelson** in 1801, and killed by a musket ball in the hour of his victory at **Trafalgar**.

followed millions of visitors, many of them pausing only briefly before their cruise ship takes them onward to new destinations, others staying longer to make the most of the north coast's many attractions.

OCHO RIOS AREA

The thriving resort centre of Ocho Rios, midway between Montego Bay and Port Antonio and almost the same distance from Kingston, has come a long way from its roots as a fishing village to become the main holiday centre and port of call for cruise ships on the north coast. With beaches on either side and plenty of sightseeing attractions nearby, Ocho Rios, known to locals as 'Ochi', is one of Jamaica's holiday favourites. The town's name means 'Eight Rivers' in Spanish, but visitors will look in vain for them. In fact, it is a corruption of *las chorreras*, Spanish for 'waterfalls' and is appropriate enough, as Jamaica's best-known scenic falls are just outside town, and smaller cascading streams are a feature of the coast east of Ocho Rios. The original village of Ocho Rios, now the downtown section of the resort with a multi-storey hotel and apartment buildings, is built around the double curve of west-facing **Ocho Rios Bay**, sheltered by a northern promontory called **The Point**.

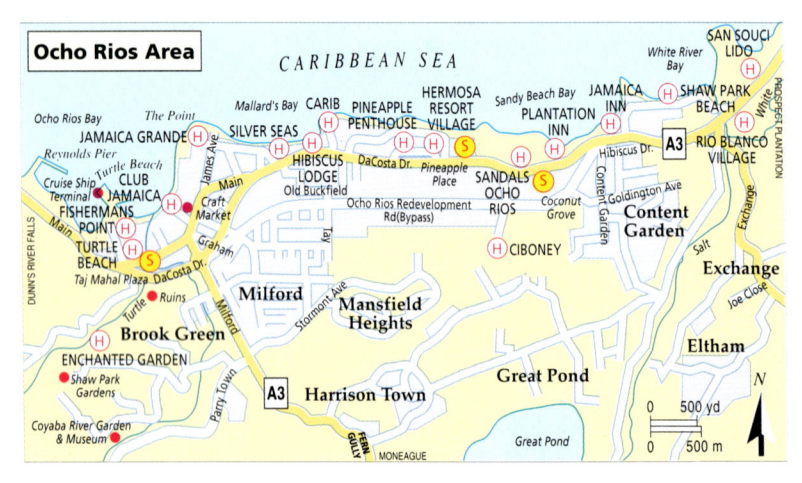

East of the city centre is the Ocho Rios **Cruise Ship Dock**, which handles a steady flow of mainly US cruise vessels. Many of their passengers are drawn as if by magnetism straight from the pier into the purpose-built complex of pricey duty-free stores immediately across the A3 highway from the cruise ship dock. A handful of resort hotels also occupy downtown sites overlooking the bay, but most of Ocho Rios's popular beach hotels are east of the city centre, spread out along the white sand beaches which stretch for kilometres along the north coast.

Above: *The modern hotels of Ocho Rios are visible from Shaw Park Gardens.*

Turtle Beach and Mallard's Bay *

Turtle Beach, immediately north of the town centre, is a half-mile (1km) stretch of urban beach dominated by the four high-rise blocks of Turtle Beach Towers, a 122-apartment condominium complex. Not the best beach in Ochi. Separated from Turtle Beach and downtown Ochi by **The Point**, the beach at **Mallard's Bay** is cleaner and a little less built up, with white sand, watersports, and the large Hibiscus Lodge hotel at its eastern end.

Shaw Park *

Just off the A3, 1 mile (1.6km) from the town centre and located on the slopes south of downtown Ocho Rios lies **Shaw Park Gardens**. This magnificent expanse of landscaped garden covers 34 acres (14ha) of tropical trees, waterfalls and flowering shrubs, and is home to many colourful bird species. There are fine views of Ocho Rios Bay and the beaches. Open 09:00–17:00.

OCHO RIOS COCKTAIL

Try this refreshing drink originating in Jamaica:
• One measure dark rum
• One measure guava juice or half cup diced guava
• Quarter measure lime juice
• 4 ice cubes
Blend all the ingredients until smooth. Serve chilled in a champagne glass.

Above: *It's the experience of getting wet that counts at Dunn's River Falls.*

Close to Shaw Park is the **Coyaba Garden and Museum**, a riverside tropical garden also to the south of Ocho Rios, which is worth a brief visit, not least for the attached museum containing Arawak relics. Open 08:30–17:00 daily.

Not much more than its descriptive name implies, **Fern Gully** is a 4-mile (7km) stretch of road which starts just two miles (3km) south of Ocho Rios and winds through a gully full of ferns.

Dunn's River Falls ★★★

Some 2 miles (3km) west of the town centre, Ochi's biggest tourist attraction is impressive although not quite as spectacular as some promoters would have you believe. The river drops some 600ft (195m) to the sea, but the falls themselves are a rather gentle series of cataracts, the highest less than 30ft (9m) high. Access to the river and the cascades is on the landward side of the A1 highway; towards the sea, the view is marred by a large bauxite plant. Open 09:00–17:00 daily.

Sandy Beach Bay and White River Bay ★★★

East of Mallard's Bay, on the A3 highway, lie Ochi's longest and best strands, as indicated by the half-dozen top resorts scattered from the west end of Sandy Beach to the east end of White River Bay. This picturesque expanse is a popular beach destination for holiday-makers and, although the gentle waters and white sands are enjoyed mostly by the well-heeled patrons of the upmarket resorts here, the beaches are indeed open to the public.

DEEP-SEA ANGLING

Jamaica is tops for deep-sea fishing, with big fish including **blue** and **white marlin, wahoo, tuna** and **dolphin** (dorado) waiting to take the bait only 15 minutes offshore, where Jamaica's reefs give way to blue ocean. Blue marlin can be caught year-round, though the best season is reckoned to be summer and autumn. The **Port Antonio Blue Marlin Tournament**, in October, is one of the Caribbean's top deep-sea angling events. Best places for boat charters are Montego Bay, Ocho Rios and Port Antonio.

The **White River** which winds its way towards the ocean is the border separating the parishes of St Ann and St Mary, and the location for a 45-minute raft ride through beautiful tropical riverside scenery, with a stop for swimming. The course of the river lies about 5 miles (8km) east of Ocho Rios centre.

Prospect Plantation *

This working plantation near Ocho Rios grows a bounty of bananas, sugarcane, coconuts and breadfruit. Visitors are able to tour the plantation fields and sample the produce on a jitney carriage tour, or on horseback, and for US$50 you can plant a tree which will bear your name, joining the ranks of famous visitors to Prospect who include Sir Noel Coward, Sir Winston Churchill and Charlie Chaplin. Tours on Monday to Saturday starting at 11:00 and 13:30, and on Sunday at 15:00.

Harmony Hall ***

For anyone with an interest in Caribbean art, Harmony Hall – on the Coast Road, just 4 miles (7km) east of downtown – is not to be missed. The attractive 19th-century building, originally the residence of a Methodist minister, is graced by typically Jamaican wooden fretwork archways and now houses the **Back Gallery**, displaying works by some of Jamaica's finest sculptors and painters, with special emphasis on the primitive and naive painters and traditional arts and crafts, and also the **Front Gallery**, which hosts a programme of exhibitions that change regularly. Open 09:00 –17:00 daily.

> **GETTING HITCHED**
>
> Jamaica is not only an ideal place for a honeymoon – you can also get married there with very little red tape. For a **civil ceremony**, you need to have been on the island for only 24 hours, and the only papers you need are your passport and birth certificate. Most tour operators can arrange a wedding and honeymoon package, as can many hotels and resorts. **Church weddings** take a little longer to organise and most wedding organisers will ask you to provide copies of the relevant documents at least six weeks ahead.

Below: *Harmony Hall features Jamaican-style fretwork archways.*

JAMES BOND

Author **Ian Fleming** invented the world's most famous spy while staying at his villa, **Goldeneye**, in Oracabessa and wrote all 13 of his Bond novels there. Looking for a name for his debonair hero, Fleming's eye lit on the spine of one of the books in his library – the authoritative **Birds of the West Indies**. The author of this tome, the real James Bond, could never have guessed that he would be immortalised as fiction's suavest, deadliest secret agent. But, then, 'The Man with the Golden Binoculars' just doesn't have the same ring, does it?

Opposite: *Largely passed by, Port Maria has not yet succumbed to tourism.*

Goshen Wilderness Resort ★

Originally a flourishing plantation, this family resort is located just beyond the outskirts of the town of Goshen, and is a popular holiday spot. Despite the suggestion of wild adventure in its name, the surrounding wilderness here is, in fact, rather tame, with no jungle or wild animals. Nevertheless, the resort offers a number of interesting diversions for the holidaymaker. The freshwater lake, for example, is stocked for sport fishing, and included among the other attractions are boat rides and a wonderful petting zoo to entertain bored offspring. Goshen Wilderness Resort makes a pleasant day out for families. Open 10:00–17:00 daily.

Goldeneye ★★

At **Oracabessa**, a small village approximately 13 miles (21km) east of Ocho Rios, Ian Fleming, the creator of James Bond, spent the winter months between 1946 and 1964. It is here, at his villa Goldeneye, that he wrote all 13 of his 007 novels, and several of the many Bond films have been shot on location in Jamaica. There are still many Fleming mementoes lying about the beach villa, but to see them you'll have to rent it, as it is not open to casual visitors (*see* At a Glance/Where to Stay *on p. 75*).

Port Maria

Port Maria, 20 miles (32km) east of Ocho Rios, is yet another former banana boom town which has fallen on hard times since the advent of bigger refrigerated cargo vessels (which its small harbour cannot handle) and roads to truck fruit to other ports. Unlike Port Antonio, which recouped its fortunes by pioneering Jamaican tourism, Port Maria has yet to become a hit with visitors to the island, despite its attractive setting on eastward-facing **Port Maria Bay**, a turquoise expanse of ocean framed by steep hills covered with woodland and plantations. The town itself has a few buildings of minor interest, but the main attractions are on the hills above and behind the port, where another of Jamaica's best-known, most-loved and talented expatriates made his home.

Among Port Maria's older buildings is **St Mary's Parish Church**. Built of limestone in 1861, it has an attractive churchyard planted with nodding palm trees. Also of note, though rather neglected, is the **St Mary Court House** which dates from 1820. Immediately opposite the courts is the **Tacky Monument**, erected in memory of the rebel slave leader Tacky, who led the Easter Rebellion of 1760 that began in St Mary parish.

Firefly ***

Firefly, the Jamaican home of composer, musician, actor and playwright Sir Noel Coward, is 1½ miles (2km) north of Port Maria. Visit for high tea or Martini cocktails on the lawn, which boasts a breathtaking view over Port Maria Bay. **Island Outpost**, which administers the house as a unique museum on behalf of its owner, the Jamaican National Heritage Trust, has restored Firefly to look just as it was on the day Coward died – Sunday, 28 February 1965. Finishing

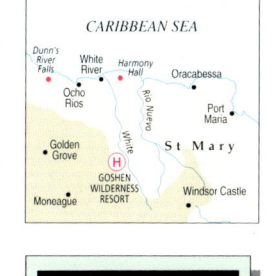

Noel Coward

Noel Coward (1899–1973) first came to Jamaica in 1950, and bought a villa which he named **Firefly** in the hills above **Port Maria** where he lived for much of the rest of his life. Famed for his dry wit and equally dry Martinis, Coward was incredibly prolific and a multi-talented actor, playwright, composer, producer, author and painter. Many of his paintings decorate the walls at Firefly, and the stunning land- and seascape surrounding the house inspired one of Coward's best-loved songs, *A Room with a View*.

> **MEET THE PEOPLE**
>
> Too many visitors meet Jamaicans only as service providers – whether waiters, taxi-drivers, watersport instructors, street vendors or ganja peddlers. To find out what Jamaicans are like at home, join the 'Meet the People' programme instituted by the **Jamaica Tourist Board**. More than 1000 Jamaican families have signed up to welcome visitors into their lives for a day or more. The programme is free to visitors, and the JTB will match you with hosts who share your interests.

touches include virtually every last detail, such as an unfinished painting by Coward on the easel in his studio and his silk dressing gown hanging on the bathroom door. One almost expects the great man, elegant as ever, to step, cocktail shaker in hand, onto the lawn. He won't, though, because he's buried under it. A plain white marble slab marks the grave. Open 09:00–17:00 daily.

Brimmer Hall ***

Five miles (8km) southwest of Port Maria, this wooden Great House is surrounded by 700 acres (280ha) of plantations where grapefruit, coconut, pimento, sugar cane and bananas are grown. Built in 1817, it is decorated with colonial antiques. Open daily; 2-hour guided tours of house and plantation start at 11:30, 13:30 and 15:30.

ST ANN'S BAY

The quiet capital of the eponymous parish is all the quieter now that it has been bypassed by the recently upgraded coast highway and, with a scattering of colonial buildings – including the 19th-century courthouse – it is a pleasant stop en route between Ocho Rios and Montego Bay. Statues of two towering figures from Jamaican history stand on the main street, in the centre of St Ann's: the bronze statue of **Columbus**, the first European to put Jamaica on the map, was cast in Genoa, Columbus's birthplace, and the **Marcus Garvey Monument** commemorates St Ann's most famous son. Born in 1887, Garvey is now considered a Jamaican national hero because of his lifelong campaign to give African-Caribbean and African-American people a sense of their African roots.

Below: *Marcus Garvey wanted to give descendants of African slaves pride in their roots.*

Seville Great House *

This plantation manor was built in 1745 from stone recycled from the first Spanish settlement on the island, Sevilla la Nueva (New Seville) which stood half a mile (1km) west of St Ann's Bay. Founded in 1509 and abandoned in 1533, the Spanish settlement provided a source of dressed stone for a number of later settlers. Seville Great House is now a museum, and in the grounds stands the estate's sugar mill, molasses boiling house and waterwheel. Open 09:00–17:00 daily.

Chukka Cove *

World-class polo, riding and show-jumping events are the main attractions at Jamaica's top equestrian centre. Chukka Cove also offers scenic horseback trails and riding packages, varying from two hours to three days of riding. Open 09:00–17:30 daily.

RUNAWAY BAY

Runaway Bay's name comes – according to some sources – from the flight of the escaping Spanish garrison following their defeat by the British in 1658. According to others, the place was favoured by runaway slaves because from here, in a stolen pirogue, it was only 90 miles (130km) to Cuba, where they might find refuge. Runaway Bay was little more than a name on the map until the development of tourism, but the fine beaches between the village itself and Salem, some 3 miles (5km) east, were bound to attract resort development, and a string of resort hotels now dominates this sector of the coast.

Cardiff Hall *

Now restored to its former glory, this Great House, 1 mile (1.6km) east of Runaway Bay, was one of the first on the island, with one of Jamaica's largest sugar estates spread around it. A tour of the mansion gives some idea of the grandeur in which the 18th-century white Jamaican planters lived. The estate has now been developed, and includes the **Runaway Bay Golf Course**. Open 09:00–17:00 daily.

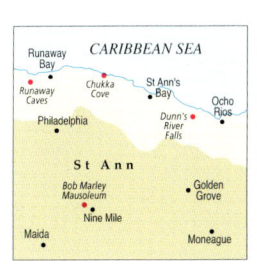

FRIENDS OF THE SEA

Non-profit organisation **Friends of the Sea**, which is dedicated to saving Jamaica's marine environment, has a list of rules for visitors to the island's seas, reefs and beaches:
• Don't touch or spear any marine life.
• Don't let your hands, feet, fins, scuba tank or boat anchor come into contact with any part of the delicate coral reef. Don't stand on coral heads.
• Don't take, or buy, starfish, conch shells, sea fans, coral or turtle products.
• Don't litter. Your trash is harmful to marine life as well as unsightly.
• Observe the closed season for lobsters – it is illegal for any restaurant to serve fresh lobster between 1 April and 30 June.

Runaway Caves **

West of Runaway Bay, en route to Discovery Bay, are limestone caverns which plunge as deep as 120ft (35m) underground. Guided tours on foot and by boat explore the partially flooded caves and their twisted stone formations. The tours include a boat trip across the underground lake known as **Green Grotto**. Tours 09:00–17:30 daily.

Bob Marley Mausoleum ***

Probably the best known Jamaican in history, Bob Marley was born at Nine Mile, 15 miles (24km) south of Runaway Bay, and was buried here following his death from a brain tumour in 1981. His mausoleum is on Mount Zion, on the site of the family home, a small wooden shack which has been rebuilt in stone in his memory. Marley's tomb, a slab of white Italian marble, is in a small chapel combining Ethiopian influences (like all Rastafarians, Marley believed in Ethiopia as his ancestral home) with pictures of Marley and his fellow Wailers, Rastafarian symbols, banners and badges. Outside is the 'inspiration stone' where Marley sat as a boy, before his family moved to Kingston when he was 13. It, and virtually everything else in the mausoleum compound, have been painted in the three symbolic colours of Rastafari – red, yellow and green. In the church, a leather funeral album contains the names of the thousands of people who joined Marley's funeral procession. Almost as many hustlers, higglers and 'guides' seem to lurk in the environs of the mausoleum. Open 08:30–17:00 daily.

Below: *A guide at the Bob Marley Mausoleum enthusiastically traces his hero's footsteps.*

DISCOVERY BAY

ORACABESSA COCKTAIL
• One measure crème de banane
• Half measure lemon juice
• One measure dark rum
• Half sliced banana
• Top up with lemonade
Shake the crème de banane, rum and lemon juice with ice and pour into a highball glass. Decorate with the sliced banana, then top with lemonade. Adorn with sliced pineapple or maraschino cherry.

Discovery Bay

The location of Discovery Bay – straddling the main coast highway, with a gigantic bauxite shipping operation dominating its stretch of waterfront and narrow beach – has not helped it to develop as a tourism destination. There is little to see, but there are small guesthouses.

Columbus Park **

This open-air museum is perched above the shore, 1 mile (1.6km) west of Discovery Bay, on the spot where Columbus is said to have made his landfall in 1494. The museum's collection is eclectic and haphazard but nevertheless fascinating, with colonial cannon, bits and pieces from the old sugar refineries – including a waterwheel – and other relics of the bygone and unlamented plantation era. Open daily, daylight hours.

Above: *Relics of Jamaica's past lie on display at Columbus Park.*
Below: *Columbus is said to have made landfall at the site of Columbus Park in 1494.*

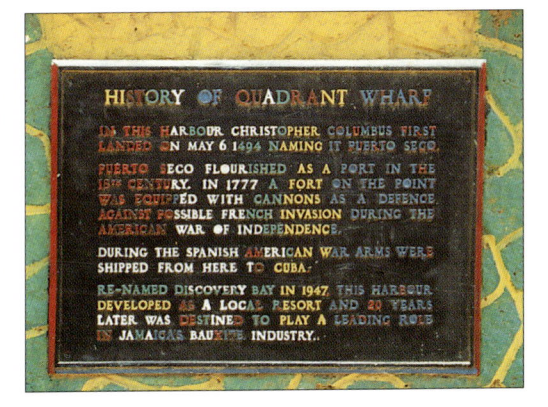

Puerto Seco Beach **

Across the road from Columbus Park, Puerto Seco is a well maintained public beach and a place to cool off if you are on an independent sightseeing outing along the north coast. The entry fee onto the gently shelving sand, offering safe, easy swimming, makes it worthwhile. Open 08:00–17:00 daily.

St Ann & St Mary at a Glance

Best Times to Visit

Like the rest of Jamaica, this region's constant moderate climate allows visits virtually any time of the year.

Getting There

The north coast highway (A1/A3) connects **Ocho Rios** with **Montego Bay** (133 miles/180km) and **Port Antonio** (66 miles/100km). **Kingston** is 54 miles (89km) south on the A1.

Getting Around

Minibus services are crowded, irregular and unsafe, but **car hire** and **taxis** are available at all resorts. All-inclusive resorts also operate airport transfers to Montego Bay and **shuttle buses** into Ocho Rios.

Where to Stay

Most accommodation on the north coast around St Mary and St Ann is in 'all-inclusive resorts' where the price of a one-week or fortnight package includes everything, from cocktails to watersports, and is excellent value. There are also conventional hotels in and around Ocho Rios, and a scattering of villas, but few budget guesthouses.

Ocho Rios
Luxury
Ciboney Ocho Rios, Main Street, PO Box 728, Ocho Rios, tel: 974 1027, fax: 974 5838. 300-room all-inclusive, 45 acres (18ha), private club, pools, hot tubs, restaurants, and bars.
Enchanted Garden, PO Box 284, Eden Bower Road, Ocho Rios, tel: 974 1400, fax: 974 5823. 110 air-con rooms, park-like grounds; many luxuries.
Jamaica Inn Hotel, Main Street (Old Road), PO Box 1, Ocho Rios, tel: 974 2514, fax: 974 2449. Small, luxury, 45 rooms, own beach at Sandy Beach Bay; restaurant and bars.
Sandals Ocho Rios, Main Street, PO Box 771, Ocho Rios, tel: 974 5691, fax: 9745700. Couples-only all-inclusive, 237 rooms, restaurants, bars, own beach on Sandy Beach Bay.
Shaw Park Beach Hotel, PO Box 17, Cutlass Bay, Ocho Rios, tel: 974 2552, fax: 974 5043. Legendary luxury, 127 air-con rooms overlooking White River Bay, tennis, watersports, pool, restaurant and three bars.

Mid-range
Comfort Suites Resort, 17 DaCosta Drive, Ocho Rios, tel: 974 8050, fax: 974 8070. Comfortable, air-con suites, cable TV, kitchenette, tennis, restaurant, bars, beach shuttle.

Budget
The Village Hotel, 54 Main Street, Ocho Rios, tel: 974 9293, fax: 9742605. Small and friendly 34-room hotel with two restaurants.
Little Pub Inn, 59 Main Street, PO Box 256, Ocho Rios, tel: 974 2324, fax: 974 5825. 21 air-con rooms, en suite, room service, restaurant; near beach, entertainment and golf.

Ocean Sands Resort, James Avenue, Ocho Rios, tel: 974 2605 (no fax). Value for money, 28-room hotel with two restaur-ants, kids under the age of 12 stay free.

Runaway Bay
Luxury
Club Caribbean, PO Box 65, Runaway Bay, St Ann, tel: 973 3507, fax: 973 3509. Good value all-inclusive,135 beach-front cottages, watersports, diving, tennis and gym, restaurant and three bars.
Hedonism III, PO Box 250, Runaway Bay, tel: 973 4100, fax: 973 2693. All inclusive resort for party animals, part of a chain with a wild reputation.
Breezes Golf and Beach Resort , PO Box 58, Runaway Bay, St Ann, tel: 973 2436, fax: 973 2352. Successful family-oriented all-inclusive.

Mid-range
Club Ambiance , PO Box 20 Runaway Bay, St Ann, tel: 973 4705, fax: 973 2067. Ocean views, health club, disco, restaurants and bars.
Franklyn D Resort, PO Box 201, Runaway Bay, St Ann, tel: 973 3070, fax: 973 3071. Family-oriented all-inclusive, 67 suites; under 16s stay free.

Budget
Caribbean Isle Hotel, PO Box 119, Runaway Bay, tel: 973 2364, fax: 974 4835. 23 air-con rooms, ocean views, pool, bar and restaurant, good service.

St Ann & St Mary at a Glance

Discovery Bay
MID-RANGE
Bay Vista Village, Queens Highway, Discovery Bay, St Ann, tel: 954 0162. 36 self-catering apartments, private beach, pool, diving, tennis, riding and golf nearby.

BUDGET
The Accommodationer, Discovery Bay, St Ann, tel: 973 2559, fax: 973 3020. Seven air-con rooms, en-suite, with room service, TV, supervised children's programme, golf, watersports, riding, near to beach and shopping.

Orcabessa and Port Maria
LUXURY
Goldeneye, Oracabessa Beach, Oracabessa, tel: 994 2282 (no fax). Ian Fleming's beach villa to rent, sleeps eight guests, staff available by prior arrangement.

MID-RANGE
Casa Maria Hotel, PO Box 10, Port Maria, tel: 994 2323, fax: 994 2324. 20 rooms on private beach, restaurants and bars.

WHERE TO EAT

Most visitors to the area stay in all-inclusive resorts or self-catering apartments. Away from Ocho Rios there are very few restaurants outside hotels, though there are plenty of fast-food outlets and jerk shacks. For places to eat away from Ochi, *see* Where to Stay.

Ocho Rios
LUXURY
Almond Tree, Hibiscus Lodge Hotel, 83–87 Main Street, tel: 974 2813. A la carte seafood, piano bar, live entertainment.
Evita's, Ocho Rios, tel: 974 2333. 19th-century mansion with Venetian cuisine, fresh pasta and delicious desserts served indoors and outdoors.
Seafood Glant, Main Street, Runaway, tel: 973 4801. Superb seafood and Jamaican cooking in the heart of Runaway Bay.

MID-RANGE
Glenn's Restaurant, Tower Cloisters, Ocho Rios, tel: 975 4360. Good value Jamaican specialities and international dishes such as pasta or burgers.
The Little Pub, 59 Main Street, Ocho Rios, tel: 974 2324. Dinner theatre with cabaret in central Georgian-style complex.

BUDGET
Ocho Rios Jerk Centre, DaCosta Drive, Ocho Rios, tel: 974 2549. The best Jamaican jerk pork, chicken and seafood in town. Very spicy.

SHOPPING

Duty-free shops opposite the **Cruise Ship Dock** just west of the Ocho Rios are stacked with luxury goods for the American cruise market – crystal glassware, jewellery, watches and fragrances. More interesting is the **Ocean Village Shopping Centre**, Turtle Beach, Ocho Rios, in the centre of town, where you can buy wood carvings, textiles, 'naive' paintings (although selling mass-produced 'native' art at whopping prices is hardly naive!) and other typically tourist tat. You'll find very much the same sort of goods, at even higher prices, in the souvenir shops within every all-inclusive resort and hotel complexes, along with swimwear, sunscreen and other beach essentials.

TOURS AND EXCURSIONS

The compulsory tour if you are staying at any of the north coast resorts is **Dunn's River Falls**, with **Jamaica Night** on the White River – a candlelit canoe ride upriver, followed by folklore show, dinner and drinks – coming a close second. All tours can be arranged through your hotel or resort representative.
The Touring Society of Jamaica, Salt Gut, Boscobel PO, St Mary, tel/fax: 975 7158. Operates a range of tours around the island, including art and architecture tours, birding expeditions, and trips into the Jamaican wilderness.

USEFUL CONTACTS

Jamaica Tourist Board, Ocean Village Shopping Centre, tel: 974 2582/3. Advice and information on sightseeing, shopping, accommodation, restaurants, tours and beaches.

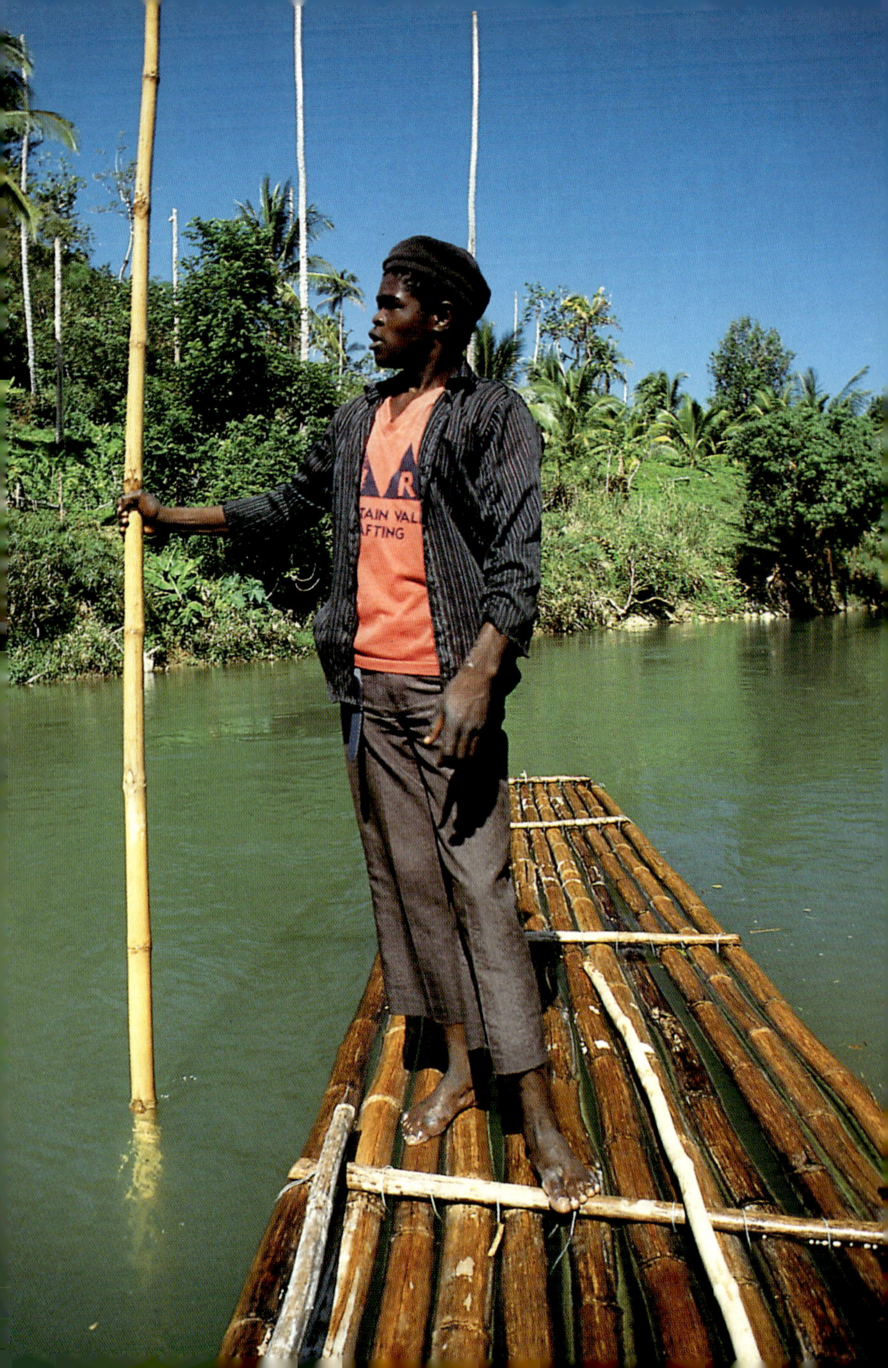
TAIN VALL
AFTING

5
St James, Trelawny and Hanover

These three counties – Hanover in the west, St James in the centre and Trelawny in the east – make up the northern half of **Cornwall**. More than any other part, this region encapsulates the extremes of Jamaican life, from its biggest resort city, **Montego Bay**, to the forest strongholds of the **Cockpit Country**, where you can still almost hear the echoes of the far from welcoming Maroon slogan: 'Me no sen', you no come'. Montego Bay (called 'Mo Bay' for short) is thronged year-round by holidaymakers from North and South America and Europe and is one of the most popular ports of call in the Caribbean. The hills inland are punctuated with hotels, villas and resorts to suit all tastes, from some of the Caribbean's most expensive properties to value-for-money all-inclusives.

Mo Bay's international airport is the preferred gateway for most holidaymakers. Most of the area's largest hotels, many of them all-inclusive, are to be found on the fine beaches of the St James coast, west of Mo Bay, while the Trelawny coast is less intensively developed. East of Mo Bay, along the Hanover coast, are a string of upmarket hideaways where you rub shoulders with the rich and famous. All around the region there are historic and purpose-built attractions to tempt you from the beach. Inland, **Hanover** and **St James** are covered by plantations and lush rolling hills, and the countryside is dotted with small farming villages. **Trelawny** parish is very different. South of the coastal plain, it rises steeply to form the rugged limestone mountains of the Cockpit Country, covered with thick jungle and still traversed by few roads.

Don't Miss

*** **Montego Bay:** beaches, shopping, and lots of nightlife, wining and dining.
*** **Montego Bay Marine Park:** scuba, snorkelling and glass-bottom boat cruises.
*** **Barnett Estate:** authentically restored plantation Great House, just outside Montego Bay.
*** **Tryall Golf Club:** one of Jamaica's top resorts, with the Caribbean's finest golf course.
** **The Great River:** the island's longest river, venue for folklore and feasting.

Opposite: *A rafter prepares for a trip down the Great River.*

MONTEGO BAY

At first sight, Jamaica's second city seems to be reserved exclusively for the business of tourism, with souvenir markets, duty-free shopping, art galleries, and a host of bars and restaurants to cater to every taste – though the prices put them out of bounds to all but a handful of Jamaicans. The first Spanish settlers, who butchered semi-wild pigs and rendered their fat into lard, called their settlement Villa Manteca (literally 'Fat City'). Since corrupted into 'Montego' Bay, the name seems appropriate for a resort that boasts Jamaica's most finely tuned tourism money-making machine.

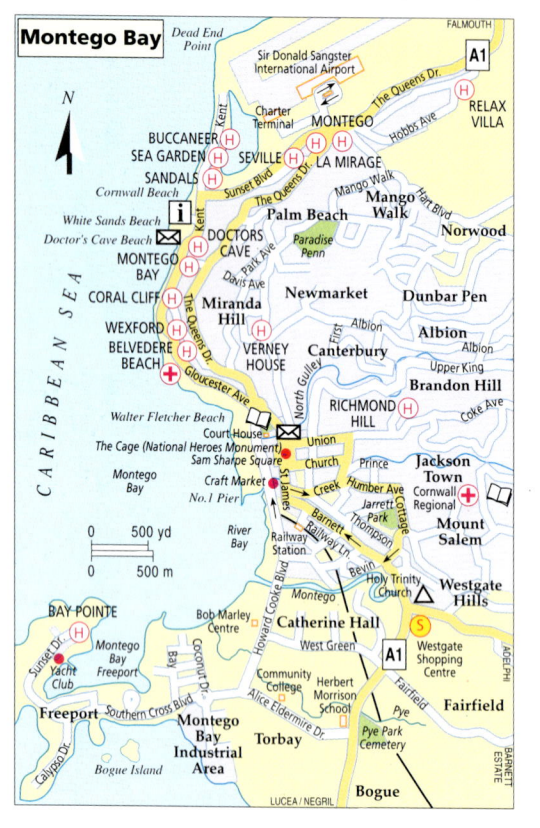

The city faces westward, overlooking the Bay, with the **Montego River** separating the city centre from the port and industrial area to the south. Montego Bay's beaches start within a mile of the city centre, and there are more than two dozen holiday hotels between central Mo Bay and Sir Donald Sangster International Airport, 2 miles (3km) north of the centre. Stretching off east along the St James coast are some of Jamaica's **best beaches** and certainly its biggest concentration of accommodation – some 40 per cent of the country's hotel rooms are in and around Montego Bay.

Montego Bay reaches a peak of excitement each August, when it hosts the annual **Reggae Sunsplash** music fest, and year round it has probably the biggest choice of nightlife on the island. Visit town on 'Monday Night Out', when Gloucester Avenue is closed to traffic and becomes a multi-flavoured celebration of spicy Jamaican food and hot Jamaican music.

Sam Sharpe Square *

Montego Bay's city plaza is named after the leader of the slave rebellion in 1831. Now a national hero, Sharpe was captured and hanged with 500 others at Montego Bay. A statue in the square depicts Sharpe and another of Jamaica's national heroes, rebel leader Paul Bogle. **The Ring**, where slaves were auctioned, and **The Cage**, where runaways and unruly sailors were locked up, are other reminders of the bad old days. Sam Sharpe Square is also the focus of a straggling street market where stallholders sell colourful souvenirs, snacks and leisurewear. But to find out what Montego Bay is really about – white sand beaches – follow Gloucester Avenue north from the city centre.

Montego Bay's Beaches ***

The first of the famed beaches is **Walter Fletcher Beach**, less than half a mile from the middle of town and more popular with local people than with tourists. It is a public beach, which means there is an admission charge and facilities including changing rooms and a snack bar. As the first in a relatively long string, however, the beach itself is just a hint of what is still to come as you head north.

Doctor's Cave Beach, about 1 mile (1.8km) from the centre, is Jamaica's first bathing beach.

> **SUNSPLASH**
>
> Invented to help put Jamaica back on the tourism map after the doldrums of the 1970s and 1980s – and to help boost visitor numbers in the summer low season – the **Reggae Sunsplash** has taken on a life of its own as one of the greatest gigs on the world music calendar, and certainly for musicians from all over the Caribbean and as far afield as the UK, South Africa and Zimbabwe. For six days and nights, with the sweet whiff of prime ganja drifting in the air, this is the place to hear reggae's biggest names – and plenty of soon-to-be-famous contenders – giving their best, and to discover what reggae is really all about.

Below: *A dynamic tribute to rebel heroes in Sam Sharpe Square.*

Above: *Marvellous Doctor's Cave Beach, Montego Bay's favourite stretch of sand, was also the first beach to be used for public bathing in Jamaica.*

Donated to Montego Bay by its last owner in 1906, the Edwardian fad for sea bathing soon brought it a genteel clientele. An admission fee is charged and there are changing rooms and a cocktail bar. Open 08:30–17:30 daily. The next beach north is **Cornwall**, where facilities are operated by the Jamaica Tourist Board, which has a Mo Bay office just across the road. The beach and the water are superb, and there is a good choice of watersports including parascending and waterskiing. Open 09:00–17:00.

Montego Bay Marine Park ***

The Marine Park comprises 10 sq miles (26km²) of sea-grass beds, coral reefs, and coastal mangrove swamp stretching from the mouth of the **Great River**, west of Montego Bay, to **Dead End Point** near the airport. Scuba and snorkelling trips and glass-bottom boat cruises are offered by a number of companies in Mo Bay.

Barnett Estate and Great House **

Built in 1735, this Jamaican manor was once the headquarters of a plantation which included almost all the land on which Mo Bay now stands. Its founder, **Colonel Nicholas Jarrett**, was one of the officers of the British force which conquered Jamaica in 1655, and his descendants, the Kerr-Jarrett family, still own and work the 3000-acre (1200ha) estate.

The **Great House** has been restored with exact attention to period detail, down to the rare books in the library and the pipes in the antique smoking cabinet. The estate has its own bar and barbecue restaurant. Open 09:00–17:00 daily.

Bob Marley Centre **

Open for frequent reggae shows and other concerts, this is the original home of the annual **Reggae Sunsplash**,

---

NOT A DOLPHIN!

Some visitors to Jamaica and the Caymans are appalled to see 'dolphin' on the menu. Don't panic – it's not a Flipper fillet. The dolphin in question is a large tropical fish, also called the **dorado** or, in the US, **mahi mahi**. With its powerful predator's body and iridescent silver colouring, it is a handsome fish and a formidable adversary for sea anglers. On the other hand, the mahi mahi has never been known to act cute, entertain children, balance balls on its nose or rescue shipwrecked mariners. And it tastes great!

the world's biggest celebration of Jamaica's own music. Held each year in August, the event lasts a full week and attracts tens of thousands of reggae fans from all over Jamaica and the world.

Montego Bay Freeport **

The manmade, hammer-shaped **Freeport Peninsula**, which forms the southern bulwark of the bay, is made from sand dredged from the seabed to create the Montego Bay Freeport, where modern container ships and gigantic cruise liners dock. Immediately opposite the gleaming **Cruise Ship Terminal**, the **Montego Freeport Shopping Centre**, with its rows of duty-free outlets, allows cruise ship passengers to be separated from their money without ever straying more than a few hundred metres from their vessel. There are sandy beaches on the seaward side of the Freeport peninsula, where the **Seawind Beach Resort** operates a private nude beach for those averse to tan lines.

ST JAMES PARISH
Rocklands Feeding Sanctuary **

This privately owned bird sanctuary lies 7 miles (12 km) west of town at Anchovy. Lisa Salmon, the owner, began feeding and caring for local birdlife 30 years ago, and hundreds of songsters now turn up for daily feeding time. The birds are so used to people that many of them will feed from your hands and, as Rocklands is almost 1000ft (300m) above sea level, you will also be rewarded by magnificent views of Montego Bay. Open 14:00–17:00 daily.

> **THE WHITE WITCH**
>
> **Rose Hall Great House**, near **Montego Bay**, is said to be haunted by **Annie Palmer**, whose first husband, John Palmer, built Rose Hall in 1770. According to legend, Annie – who had learned *obeah* from one of her slaves – first poisoned John, then went on to stab her second husband and strangle her third before taking a succession of slave lovers, whom she also murdered one by one, until the slaves finally rebelled and murdered her in 1833. Though there was a real Annie Palmer, there's not a shred of evidence to support this colourful story.

Below: *The Montego River separates Montego Bay centre from the port.*

PLANTATION LIFE

The white planters lived well, and each sugar estate was virtually a self-sufficient little kingdom surrounding the palatial great house. The working part of the estate housed the overseer and his staff, while slaves lived in streets of barrack-like quarters. If the planter was king, his white aides and artisans – bookkeepers, lawyers and overseers, farriers, masons, coopers and stillmen – were princes who could behave much as they wished where slaves were concerned. House and garden slaves often had European blood, and are said to have considered themselves superior to field slaves. The planters' great wealth bought them enormous political influence in London to help protect their way of life.

Opposite: *Greenwood Great House houses a fine collection of artworks and antiques.*

Belvedere Estate **

This working plantation 12 miles (17km) south of Montego Bay covers more than 1000 acres (405ha), most of them covered with citrus and spice plantations. With its brooks and cascading waterfalls, it's a pleasant – and cool – way to escape from the hustle of Montego Bay. Open 10:00–15:30 Monday–Saturday.

Rose Hall Great House ***

About 3 miles (5km) east of Montego Bay, this is the most famous of Jamaica's great plantation manor houses – partly because it is the closest to Montego Bay and is the one that everyone visits, having been restored from its ruined state (it was abandoned between around 1830 and 1966) as a tourist attraction. The house is furnished with fine antiques and guided tours are available every 15 minutes during the day. The gracefully proportioned Georgian structure has the requisite spine-chilling ghost story attached to it, but the version you will hear from your tour guide has barely a shred of truth in it. Open 09:00–18:00 daily.

Greenwood Great House ***

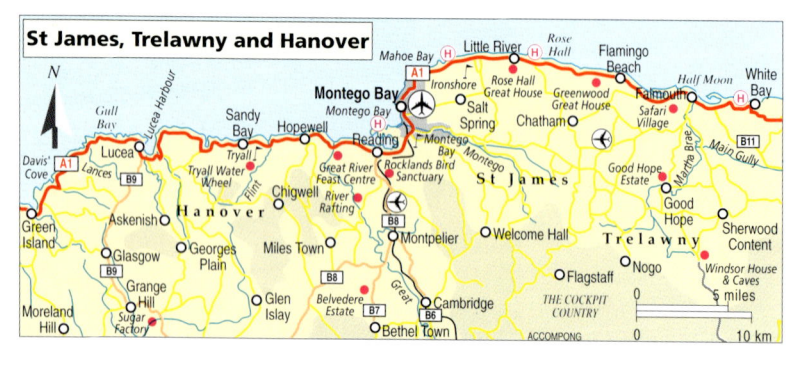

Built by the wealthy Browning family (from which the poetess **Elizabeth Barrett Browning** came), Greenwood is about 4 miles (7km) east of Montego Bay and boasts the best collection of antiques and artworks of any of the island's surviving Great Houses. It also has a fine collection of beautiful musical instruments, including a magnificent rosewood piano commissioned by Edward VII. The house was built in the late 18th century, and tours of the house and surrounding plantation are available, led by guides dressed in period costume. Open 09:00–18:00 daily.

Falmouth

The heyday of this little harbour town – on the A1 north coast highway, 14 miles (23km) east of Montego Bay – was during the sugar boom of the late 18th century, when it grew into a thriving port graced by fine public and private buildings in Georgian style. Many of these survive, and indeed Falmouth today has Jamaica's best-preserved collection of buildings from this era. **Market Street**, in the town centre, is dotted with them. The most distinguished architectural survivals include the **Methodist Manse**, built in 1799 by the wealthy Barrett family; the 18th-century **Post Office**, and the early 19th-century **Courthouse**, fronted by doric columns and a final double external staircase but somewhat marred by a clumsy restoration after a fire in the 1920s.

Jamaica Safari Village *

Just 2 miles (1km) west of Falmouth on the A1, the main attraction of this purpose-built village are the captive-bred Jamaican crocodiles, which start out as cute bug-eyed critters about 6 inches (15cm) long and eventually grow into 7ft (2m) monsters – if they don't end up as handbags, belts or shoes. Also on show are birds, snakes, and cuddlier creatures at the petting zoo. In addition, there is a snack bar and jerk centre. Open 08:30–18:00 daily.

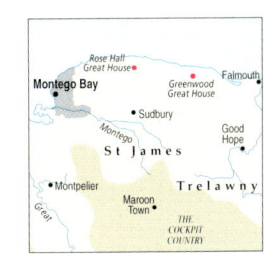

MANATEE

It's hard to credit the ungainly manatee as the supposed inspiration for the legendary **mermaid**. Only about 100 of these harmless aquatic herbivores are believed to survive in Jamaican waters – most of them around the less-developed, swampy shores of the southeast. Growing up to 10ft (3m) long, manatees are still occasionally hunted for meat and, while there are legends of manatees rescuing shipwrecked sailors, some Jamaicans also believe a manatee swimming past a boat or house can render men and women infertile.

Above: *Crocodiles sunbathe at the Jamaica Safari Village.*

> **THE DOCTOR BIRD**
>
> Jamaica's national bird is also one of its smallest. You'll see the **streamertail hummingbird** (*Trochilus polytmus*), or 'Doctor Bird', zipping around flower gardens or sipping nectar from flowers and feeder stations. Only 4½ inches (11.5cm) long without its streamer-like, 10 inch (25cm) tailfeathers, the male Doctor Bird's body is iridescent green, its crown and tail black, and its beak red. The female is less brightly coloured, without the streaming tail. Like other hummingbirds, the streamertail can hover in midair, fly straight up, down, sideways, and even go into reverse. Its in-flight hum is generated by wings which beat at almost 80 times every second when hovering – and up to 200 times per second in courtship display.

Martha Brae River ★★★

The Martha Brae flows out of the **Cockpit Country** hills to meet the Caribbean east of Falmouth. Trips down the river on a 30ft (10m) bamboo raft take about 75 minutes, ending at **Rafter's Village**, where there is a restaurant, bar, pool and shops.

Good Hope Estate ★★

This one-acre coconut and cattle plantation, 4 miles (7km) south of Falmouth, has marked trails for riding. **Good Hope Great House** was built in 1755 and, like so many of the sugar planters' mansions, fell into disuse in the early 20th century as the value of sugar dropped and the old plantation lifestyle ceased to be feasible. Good Hope was once the largest plantation on the island, covering 10,000 acres (4050ha). The estate has now been reduced to about 200 acres (80ha), but the Great House has taken on a new lease of life as a luxury hotel. With its fine Palladian architecture and Adam interior, the house must be one of the most attractive places to stay in Jamaica. Open 09:00–16:00 daily.

THE COCKPIT COUNTRY

Most of southern Trelawny parish is almost trackless wilderness. South of route B10 lies an area of almost 100 sq miles (260km^2) of virtually trackless hill country, rising at its highest point, Cockpit Peak, to 2453ft (800m).

The Land of Look Behind ★

This is the home of the **Maroons**, the proud descendants of slaves of the Spanish who took to the woods and hills from the earliest days of European settlement and proved stubbornly hard for the British colonial forces to subdue. Looking at the Cockpit Country today, it's not hard to see why. The soft, porous limestone of this part of the island has sunk into a series of crater-like hollows, the so-called 'cockpits', interspersed with steep river gorges and choked with tropical vegetation. From their hill villages, the Maroons defied all who came against them. Their slogan came to be 'Me no sen', you no come', and in the 18th and early 19th centuries only the foolish went into this territory without a promise of safe conduct from the Maroon chiefs. Not for nothing is it still called the Land of Look Behind. The main Maroon settlement is at Accompong (*see* Westmoreland and St Elizabeth *on p. 98*).

Windsor Cave **

Unlike other, more easily reached caverns on the Jamaica coast, the Windsor Cave complex has not yet been seriously commercialised – although local 'guides' who hang around the entrance will expect a hefty tip for lighting your way with a bamboo torch and may be angry if you refuse their services. The small entrance leads into a two-mile (3km) labyrinth of limestone formations – take your own reliable flashlight, and be warned that this is no place for people with a fear of bats! The cave complex has not yet been fully charted, but is believed to be the source of the **Martha Brae River**, which reaches the sea near Falmouth. Open daily, no set hours.

HANOVER PARISH

West of Montego Bay, the coast of Hanover parish lacks the long beaches of the Mo Bay area, but is dotted with elegant resorts on private coves or on landscaped hillsides. Between **Sandy Bay** and **Lucea**, the biggest town in the parish, the Hanover coast is dominated by jagged cliffs, making Lucea's natural harbour a welcome sight for local fishermen.

> **ANANSI STORIES**
>
> One of the most enduring of Jamaica's original African traditions is the myth of **Anansi**, the cunning spider who usually gets the better of his adversaries – while never quite winning conclusively. The Anansi tales, and Anansi himself, originate in Ghana (formerly the **Gold Coast**, whence many slaves were brought). The dialect they are told in is peppered with words from several West African languages – and the same stories are told too in Ghana today. Among American slaves, Bra' (Brother) Anansi became Br'er Rabbit, and 'Please don't throw me into the briar patch' is a typical Anansi stratagem.

Below: *The Martha Brae River runs down from the wild Cockpit Country.*

> **NATIONAL FLOWER**
>
> Jamaica's national flower is the tiny purple blossom of the **lignum vitae** (tree of life), a small tree which flowers in July, heralding the beginning of the hot and humid hurricane season. In earlier times, the tree was highly valued – its sticky sap was said to be a panacea for many ills, and its heavy, water-resistant wood was widely used in ship-building and engineering.

The Great River **

Flowing out of the limestone mountains of the hinterland, the Great River forms the parish boundary between **Hanover** and **St James**. To visitors accustomed to rivers on a European or North American scale, the name may seem inappropriate – the Great River is little over 50ft (15m) at its widest, but it is nevertheless the largest watercourse in the country. Lively night-time events – rum cocktails, dinner and a Jamaican folklore show – are held at the **Great River Feast Centre** close to the coast and, during the day, you can float downriver on a bamboo raft.

Tryall Golf Club ***

Jamaica's finest golf course, 12 miles (19km) west of Montego Bay, is on the site of a 19th-century sugar plantation, but immaculately groomed greens have taken the place of waving sugar cane. Tryall is respected by top golf professionals, who gather here each year to compete for golf's richest prize, the US$ 2.7 million World Championship. Tryall also offers some of Jamaica's most expensive and exclusive accommodation and a welcome mile-long (1.5km) beach.

Below: *Tryall's water wheel, built 200 years ago to power plantation machinery, still turns today though it is no longer operational.*

Tryall Water Wheel *

Tryall's most impressive historic landmark is the huge wood and cast-iron water wheel, a relic of the heyday of sugar when water was the major power source for plantation machinery. Built 200 years ago to harness the flow of the **Flint River**, the wheel still continues to turn, although it no longer powers anything.

Left: *Buildings of interest in the quiet town of Lucea include the courthouse, with its wooden clocktower and rounded cupola.*

LUCEA

Hanover's capital of Lucea is a little town of wooden buildings with shaky-looking balconies and covered arcades. About 25 miles (40km) west of Mo Bay, the original sugar port is now the hub of farm land growing bananas, pimento, ginger, yams and sugar. There is little tourism here – most visitors usually only pass through on their way from Montego Bay to Negril – but there are some historic buildings of interest.

Fort Charlotte *

Lucea's original reason for existing was its location on the only decent anchorage on this stretch of coast, and this pocket-sized fortress was built to command and defend it. Overlooking Lucea harbour, the eight-sided fort mounted 20 cannon but never had occasion to fire them except on ceremonial occasions. Open daylight hours only.

Anglican Church *

The 18th-century church is one of Jamaica's oldest and contains a neo-classical monument to **Simon Clarke**, one of the wealthiest planters of the time, by the sculptor John Flaxman. Open daily.

FLORA AND FAUNA

Jamaica has some 3000 plant species, of which at least 800 are unique to the island, including hundreds of **orchids** and almost 600 species of **fern**. Wildlife is less varied, and many Jamaican species – the **manatee**, **crocodile**, **iguana** and **yellow boa** – are listed as endangered, along with several **bird** species. There's plenty of birdlife, from **jungle parrots** to the vicious-looking **man of war** or **frigate** bird with its huge wingspan and razor beak, and the **'John Crow'**, or turkey buzzard, which despite its loathsome appearance does a good job of clearing the garbage from village middens, roadsides and beaches. At night, look out for 'rat-bats' as Jamaicans call **bats**, of which there are 25 species.

St James, Trelawny & Hanover at a Glance

BEST TIMES TO VISIT

Jamaica's climate is moderate year-round, but the heat and humidity May–November, along with seasonal rains, make it officially off-season.

GETTING THERE

Air Jamaica, **British Airways** and US carriers fly to **Donald Sangster International** (Mo Bay) with internal flights to Kingston, Negril, Port Antonio and international flights. Cruise ships dock at Mo Bay's **Cruise Ship Terminal**. **A1 highway** connects Mo Bay with Ocho Rios, Kingston and Negril.

GETTING AROUND

Resorts out of town operate shuttle **minibuses** to Mo Bay. **Taxis** run a fixed-fare system – agree the fare before boarding. Most resorts offer free or subsidised airport **transfers**.

WHERE TO STAY

Mo Bay area boasts 40% of Jamaica's hotel beds, including all-inclusives and beach resorts (St James and Trelawny) and upmarket hotels (Hanover).

Montego Bay
LUXURY

Casa Blanca Beach Club, PO Box 469, Montego Bay, tel: 952 0720, fax: 952 1424. Ocean-front rooms and suites, restaurant, dining terrace, bars, pools, private beach.
Sandals Inn, PO Box 412, Kent Avenue, Montego Bay, tel: 952 4140, fax: 952 6913. Intimate couples-only 52-room all-inclusive; emphasis on personalised service.
Sandals Montego Bay, Kent Avenue, tel: 952 5510, fax: 952 0816. 244-room all-inclusive, sports, restaurants, bars, disco.

MID-RANGE

Belvedere Beach Hotel, 33 Gloucester Avenue, Montego Bay, tel: 952 0593, fax: 979 0498. Small but close to town.
Blue Harbour Hotel, PO Box 212, Sewell Avenue, Montego Bay, tel: 952 5445, fax: 952 8930. 24-rooms, restaurant and bar, close to town.
Doctors Cave Beach Hotel, PO Box 94, Montego Bay, tel: 952 4355, fax: 952 5204. Near beach, tennis, golf, riding, and Mo Bay markets; bar, restaurants, Coconut Grove restaurant is recommended.
El Greco Resort, 11 Queens Drive, PO Box 1624, Montego Bay, tel: 940 6116, fax: 940 6115. Apartment hotel opposite Doctor's Cave Beach, fully equipped kitchens, maid service, satellite TV, pool and tennis.
Montego Bay Club Resort, Gloucester Avenue, tel: 952 4310, fax: 952 4639. Hotel near Doctor's Cave Beach; studios, suites; bars, restaurant, tennis, supermarket, boutiques.

BUDGET

Blue Harbour Hotel, Sewell Avenue, Montego Bay, tel: 952 5445, fax: 952 8930. 22-room hotel, comfortable with pool and entertainment nightly.
La Mirage, 6 Queen's Drive, Montego Bay, tel: 952 4637 Good value, 21-room hotel, kids under 12 stay free. Pool and restaurant.

St James and Trelawny Coast
LUXURY

The Atrium at Ironshore, PO Box 604, Ironshore, Montego Bay, tel: 953 2605, fax: 952 5641. Serviced apartments in gardens; restaurant and bar.
Grand Lido Braco, Rio Bueno PO, Trelawny, tel: 954 0000, fax: 954 0020. 180-room all-inclusive, tennis, golf course, biggest pool in the Caribbean.
Coyaba Beach Resort and Club, Mahoe Bay, Little River, St James, tel: 953 9150, fax: 953 2244. Full-service, owner-operated; 50 luxury rooms, private beach, restaurants, bars.
Good Hope Great House, PO Box 50, Trelawny, tel/fax: 954 3289. Luxurious, 10 rooms, gardens, pool, tennis, stables.
Half Moon Golf, Tennis and Beach Club, PO Box 80, Rose Hall, Montego Bay, tel: 953 2211, fax: 953 2731. Excellent sport facilities.
Holiday Inn Hotel, PO Box 480, Rose Hall, Montego Bay, tel: 953 2485, fax: 953 2840. Luxury all-inclusive; 516 refurbished rooms.
Wyndham Rose Hall Golf and Beach Resort, PO Box 999, Rose Hall, Montego Bay, tel: 953 2650, fax: 953 2617. Luxury, 18-hole golf course, Crusoe's restaurant is excellent.

St James, Trelawny & Hanover at a Glance

Sandals Royal Caribbean, Mahoe Bay, PO Box 167, tel: 952 2331. Superb facilities; properties at other resorts, including Montego Bay area.

MID-RANGE
Cariblue Beach Hotel, PO Box 610, Ironshore, tel: 953 2250, fax: 953 2550. Good value, 20 air-con rooms, watersports, restaurant and two bars.

Hanover Coast
LUXURY
Round Hill Hotel and Villas, Hopewell, PO Box 64, Montego Bay, tel: 952 5150, fax: 952 2505. Chic rooms or villas, private beach, restaurant.
Tryall Golf, Tennis and Beach Resort. Elegant complex, 47 rooms and 49 villas on hillside; golf course, private beach, restaurants and bars.

WHERE TO EAT

Most visitors eat at their hotels, but some restaurants offer a free transfer service to tempt you from your hotel. There is little variety beyond Mo Bay.

LUXURY
Cascade Room (The Pelican), Gloucester Avenue, tel: 952 3171. Seafood, free transfer.
Norma's on the Wharf, Reading, Montego Bay, tel: 979 2745. Caribbean gourmet food, great waterside location.
Pier 1, Howard Cooke Blvd, Montego Bay, tel: 952 2452. Fine lobster, other seafood and European dishes.
Town House, 16 Church Street, Montego Bay, tel: 952 2660. Seafood and continental cuisine in elegant surroundings.
Georgian House Restaurant, 2 Orange Street, Montego Bay, tel: 952 0632. International cuisine and Jamaican seafood.

MID-RANGE
Greenhouse Restaurant, Gloucester Avenue (next to Doctors Cave Beach Hotel), tel: 952 7838. Pizza, burgers, Jamaican specials.
Native Restaurant, 7 Queens Drive, Montego Bay, tel: 979 2769. Jamaican nouvelle cuisine.
The Pelican, Gloucester Avenue, tel: 952 3171. Local dishes, seafood; free transfers.
Margueritaville Caribbean Bar and Grill, Gloucester Ave., tel: 952 4777. Beer, burgers, live music, complimentary shuttle service for dinner, 52 different marguerita's.

BUDGET
Gloucester Avenue fast foods: **Burger King**, **Shakey's Pizza**, **KFC** and **McDonald's**.
Native Jerk and **Garden Bar**, 56 Market Street, tel: 979 5063. Hot, spicy jerk dishes.
The Pork Pit, Gloucester Avenue, tel: 952 1046. Jerk chicken, pork and fish.

SHOPPING

Three **craft markets** (Cornwall Beach, Walter Fletcher Beach, Number One Pier) sell beachwear, local crafts and 'naive' paintings (licensed vendors at all three). Duty-free complexes at **Montego Bay Freeport Cruise Ship Terminal**.

TOURS AND EXCURSIONS

Appleton Estate Express Tour, St Elizabeth, tel: 963 9215 (no fax). Day tour of the island's biggest rum distillery and sugar plantations.
Evening On The Great River, Unity Hall, Great River, Mo Bay, tel: 952 5097 (no fax). Boat ride up torch-lit river, followed by dinner and folklore show.
Mountain Valley Rafting, Lethe, Montego Bay, tel: 912 0020 (no fax). One-hour rafting trip on the Great River.
Accompong Maroon Tour, 32 Church Street, Montego Bay, tel: 952 4546 Tours of Accompong Town and St Elizabeth with visits to a bush doctor, Jamaican lunch and Maroon singers and dancers.
CUBA: Several weekly flights (1hr) and many companies operate excursions to Havana.
Caribic Vacations, Gloucester Avenue, Montego Bay, tel: 952 5013, fax: 952 0981.
Sunholiday Travel & Tours, PO Box 531, Montego Bay, tel: 953 2391, fax: 979 0725.

USEFUL CONTACTS

Jamaica Tourist Board, Cornwall Beach, tel: 952 4425.
Jamaica Union of Travellers Association, Claude Clarke Avenue, Norwood, PO Box 1155, Montego Bay, tel: 979 0778, fax: 952 0813. Transfers, taxis, sightseeing, shopping.

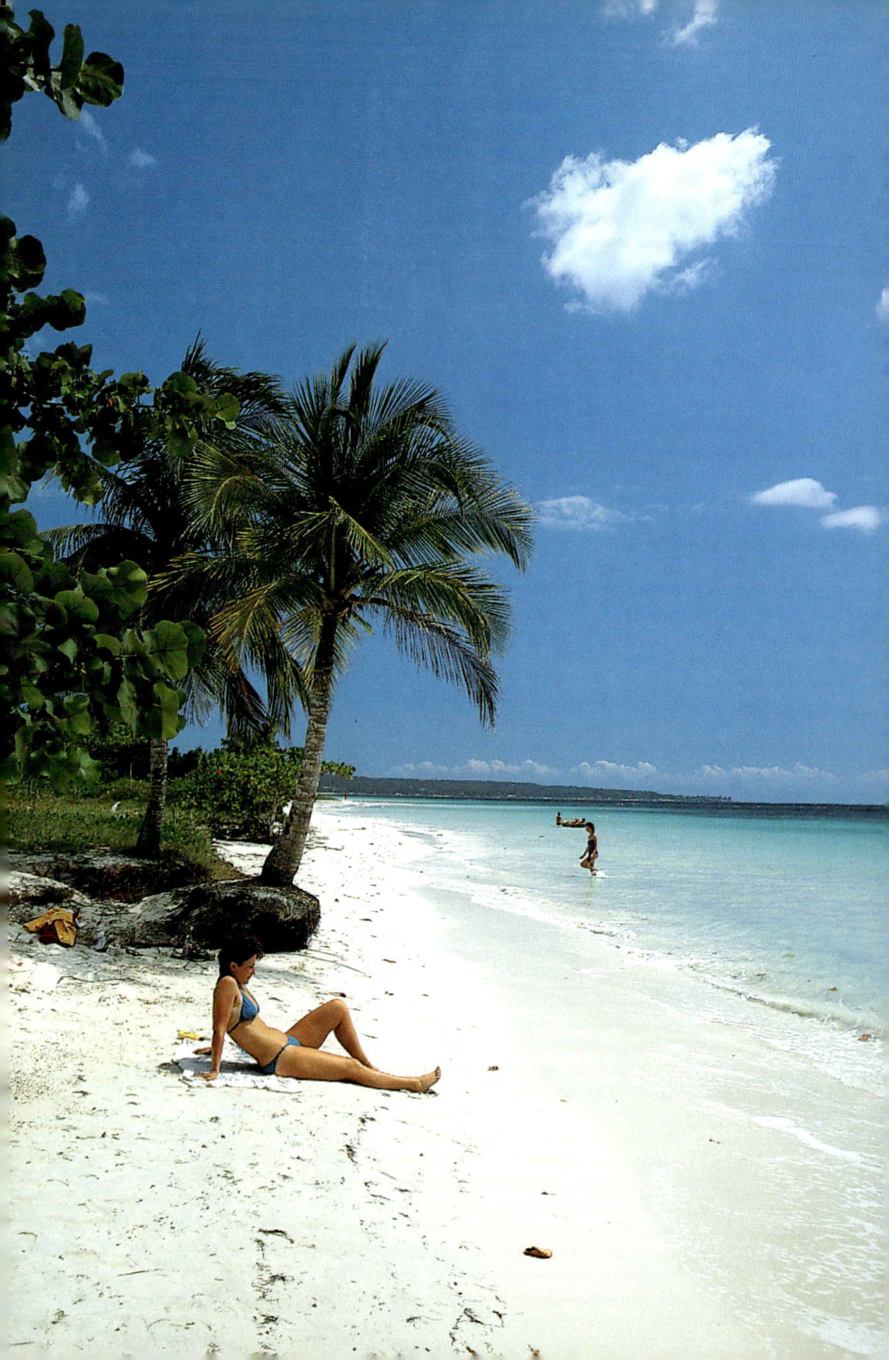

6
Westmoreland and St Elizabeth

Cornwall county's two southern parishes are very different from their north coast neighbours. **Negril**, on the very western tip of the island, is a thriving, fun-loving holiday resort, which started life as a tiny rivermouth fishing hamlet, became a backpacker's mecca in the 1960s, and then a fully-fledged tourism destination in the 1980s. But the small towns and villages spread out along the south coast are far less developed, with only a scattering of hotels and guesthouses at **Bluefields** on the **Westmoreland** coast and **Black River** and **Treasure Beach** in **St Elizabeth**. This slow pace of growth is due to the relative inaccessibility of the two parishes, with the impenetrable Cockpit Country separating St Elizabeth from Trelawny parish to the north, and a rather winding and pot-holed coastal road connecting Negril and the south coast with Montego Bay.

Sightseeing attractions in Westmoreland and in St Elizabeth are generally natural or cultural rather than purpose-built. Nevertheless, most people heading for this area seek a beach holiday. Westmoreland's southern coastline is rocky and inaccessible for much of its length, but the parish's short stretch of west coast, which includes Jamaica's westernmost point, is occupied by **Negril Beach**, a 7-mile (11km) stretch of irresistible white sand. St Elizabeth, east of Westmoreland, is bound in the north by the wilderness of the Cockpit Country, and the northern part of the parish is the home of Jamaica's biggest **Maroon** community.

DON'T MISS

*** **Negril:** laid-back resort with the best beach in Jamaica.
*** **Black River:** venture into the **Great Morass** to see crocodiles, egrets and wild wetlands.
*** **YS Falls:** waterfalls tumble through lush woodland on this working cattle farm.
** **Bamboo Avenue:** century-old giant bamboos shade miles of highway.
** **Appleton Estate:** see how fine rum is made and sample the product.

Opposite: *Negril's magnificent beach stretches for 7 miles (11km).*

Above: *A gentle evening cruise by sail past Negril Beach; the western extremity of Jamaica is renowned for its stunning sunsets.*

Although most of the town of Negril lies within Westmoreland, the parish line dividing Hanover and Westmoreland passes through Negril, and Negril Airport, Bloody Bay, part of Negril Beach and many of Negril's resorts and restaurants are technically part of Hanover.

NEGRIL

Magnificent sunsets, non-stop fun, and a youthful holiday clientele are the hallmarks of Jamaica's most westerly resort. This once tiny fishing settlement takes a little longer to get to than most other resort areas, and until fairly recently it was inaccessible enough to deter most visitors and developers. The stretch of white sand that makes Negril so popular now was one of the last Jamaican strands to be developed for tourism and, as late as the mid-1970s, this was a refuge for a handful of those in the know seeking a more relaxed getaway than offered by the big and bustling north coast resorts. Laid-back reggae and a whiff of ganja are still a part of the Negril scene, but the small, family-run guesthouses which were the pioneers of Negril tourism are gradually being ousted by bigger hotels, and there are few empty stretches on the sands of **Long Bay**.

Negril village proper is no more than a couple of streets with banks, shops, a tourist office, travel agencies and a few bars and restaurants on the south bank of the **Negril River**, which provides a sheltered anchorage for fishing boats. A long strip of tourist establishments continues south through the **West End** district to **South Negril Point**, where a lighthouse warns shipping away from the cliffs. A clutch of hotels, restaurants and guesthouses perches atop the cliffs, with views west over the Caribbean, and gathering to watch the spectacular sunset is a nightly ritual.

Negril's – and, indeed, Jamaica's – best beach starts north of the Negril River and stretches the length of Long Bay to **Rutland Point**, which separates Long Bay from a separate, smaller beach at **Bloody Bay**, once a pirate refuge. Hotels and guesthouses run along this whole stretch. Inland, a vast expanse of swampland known as the **Great Morass** is fast being drained and developed as Negril's tourism boom gathers pace. Negril is the place to go for the ultimate barefoot beach holiday, with fantastic sands, lots of watersports above and below the surface, lively nightlife and a great choice of places to stay, eat, and drink.

Development

Arguably, the area is showing some growing pains. The demands of tourism are stretching Negril's infrastructure to – and sometimes beyond – its limits, and improvements to roads, water supply, sewerage and electricity supply can cause the occasional hiccup. That said, Negril's developers claim they are determined not to repeat the excesses of tourism development elsewhere, and the town's building code aims to keep buildings below the height of the tallest palm tree, while extensive environmental studies are required before new construction is permitted. Offshore, Negril has more to offer snorkellers and scuba divers than most Jamaican resorts, with a long and well-preserved reef not far offshore. Though fishing and pollution resulting from attempts to drain the Negril wetlands have damaged the reef environment, parts of the reef have now been declared marine parks and efforts are being made to safeguard the marine life.

> **CALICO JACK**
>
> **Negril** was a favourite pirate anchorage, and some say the pirates' nasty habits gave **Bloody Bay** its name (though it more likely came from the whalers who butchered their catch here). **John Rackman**, or 'Calico Jack' (he got his name from his fondness for calico underwear), made it his base until 1726, when he was captured by **Captain Jonathan Barnet** of the Royal Navy and sent to the gallows at Port Royal. Among his crew were two female buccaneers, **Anne Bonney** and **Mary Read**, who by all accounts were just as tough as some of their crewmates.

Below: *The coast around Negril's West End is rocky, with cliffs reaching down to the blue sea.*

Above: *Prized for its superb powder-like sand, Negril Beach is kept clean.*
Opposite: *The lighthouse at Negril affords marvellous views.*

ARTIFICIAL REEFS

After a seven-year campaign, funds were granted to create the **Negril Marine Park** in 1996. The **Negril Coral Reef Preservation Society** already has 36 permanent reef mooring buoys in **Long Bay** so that boats no longer anchor on the reef. Jamaica is also in the forefront of a high-tech coral reef regeneration project. Marine biologists have discovered that corals can be persuaded to take root and grow faster on a metal framework if a trickle of electric current is passed through it to speed up mineral deposits from surrounding seawater.

Negril Beach ***

As the finest beach in Jamaica, Negril Beach deserves every one of its three stars here. While many of Jamaica's most attractive strands have been privatised by upmarket hotels or turned into city-operated pay beaches, Negril's is still open to all. Its 7-mile (11km) expanse of white coral sand is lined by hotels, guesthouses, food shacks, cocktail bars and more sophisticated restaurants, and the horizon is dotted with the sails of fishing boats, windsurfers, catamarans and cruising yachts. Every watersport under the sun is on offer. Along the beach, peddlers sell everything the visitor could wish for – from fresh coconuts and pineapple chunks to sunscreen, ganja and extra-large cigarette papers – and there's a rock-steady soundtrack of dub, reggae and roots rock day and night.

You can eat and drink in a different spot at every meal for a fortnight and still have new places to visit, and – despite Negril's rapid growth into a full-fledged resort – the atmosphere is distinctly more laid-back than in any other Jamaican resort. Tourism has become a way of life. The beach is patrolled by plainclothes police officers on electric golf carts, and while a late night stroll is not advisable, you can stroll along the beach for miles during the day and evening without significant hassle.

At the south end of Negril Beach, just across the river from the village centre, the market vendors sell carved ornaments, beachwear, weaving, artwork and snacks. Open 08:00 to sunset daily.

Booby Cay ★★

At the north end of Negril Beach, **Rutland Point** juts out into the Caribbean, separating **Long Bay** from smaller **Bloody Bay**, a palm-fringed crescent of sand which once provided an anchorage and careenage for buccaneers such as the renowned Calico Jack Rackham – and for whalers, who butchered their catch here, giving the bay its rather gruesome name. Just offshore, the tiny island of Booby Cay is like the typical desert island depicted in cartoons – just a few boulders, a ring of sand, and a cluster of lonely palm trees. Used as a location for Disney's version of *20,000 Leagues under the Sea*, it is named for the gannet-like booby birds which once nested there. You can rent a canoe, sailboat or jet ski at Negril Beach to visit the island, which offers good snorkelling around its rocky shores, or take a half-day sailing cruise from Negril.

Negril Lighthouse ★

Just south of the cliffs of **South Negril Point**, the red-and-white-striped lighthouse was built in 1836, when its lantern ran on paraffin. This is Negril's only historic site, although the view from the westernmost point of the island is more impressive than the lighthouse itself. Open by special arrangement only; contact the Jamaican Tourist Board in Negril.

WESTMORELAND PARISH
Savanna-La-Mar

Unfortunately, the Westmoreland parish capital of Savanna-La-Mar, 18 miles (28km) east of Negril, has fallen on rather hard times and its dilapidated buildings (which were hit hard by Hurricane Gilbert in September 1988) are a sad contrast to Negril's tourism-driven prosperity. Without a beach, 'Sav', as it is affectionately known by the local inhabitants, is unlikely ever to rival thriving Negril. Although there is little to divert the visitor passing through, the town provides an interesting look at a different Jamaica.

VANISHING WETLANDS

Inland from Negril's seven miles of sandy beach lies a less well-known environmental asset – the 6000-acre (2430ha) wetland known as the Great Morass (there are two wetland areas with this name, one at Negril, the second inland from Black River). Fed by the **Orange** and **Fish** rivers, the swamplands are a giant filter, absorbing the silt that washes down off the hills, and protecting Negril's coral reef from being stifled under gallons of mud.

> **ROYAL PALMS**
>
> Among Jamaica's most striking trees is the graceful royal palm, an emblem of the island for many visitors. The world's largest concentration of Jamaican royal palms is within the Great Morass outside Negril (not to be confused with the Great Morass by the Black River) where a 250-acre (100ha) expanse of wetlands has been set aside as a reserve. The reserve there was created in the early 1980s after an upsurge of popular protest against plans by the owner, the **Petroleum Corporation of Jamaica**, to use it for peat-mining. It is now managed as a protected conservation area by the **Negril Environmental Protection Trust**.

Bluefields **

This small fishing village spread out along a curve of pebbly beach approximately 15 miles (24km) east of the capital at Savanna-La-Mar has attracted a trickle of refugees from the days when Negril was known as a tranquil hippy haven, and is still determined to escape full-scale tourism. There are a handful of family-run guesthouses and restaurants in Bluefields, but this is essentially Jamaica for determined escapists who are living on a budget.

Shafston Estate Great House *

This historic Great House, lovingly restored in 1992 and now run as a comfortable guesthouse, is situated just 1½ miles (2km) from the vilage of Bluefields on a hillside site among pimento plantations, with fine views and wide variety of birds and plants.

Seaford Town *

About 25 miles (40km) northeast of Savanna-La-Mar, this is a tiny inbred community of white Jamaicans descended from German settlers who came to Jamaica in the 1830s. Refusal to intermarry with black neighbours has led to the decline and imminent extinction of this eccentric group, who once numbered more than a thousand but are now down to less than 200.

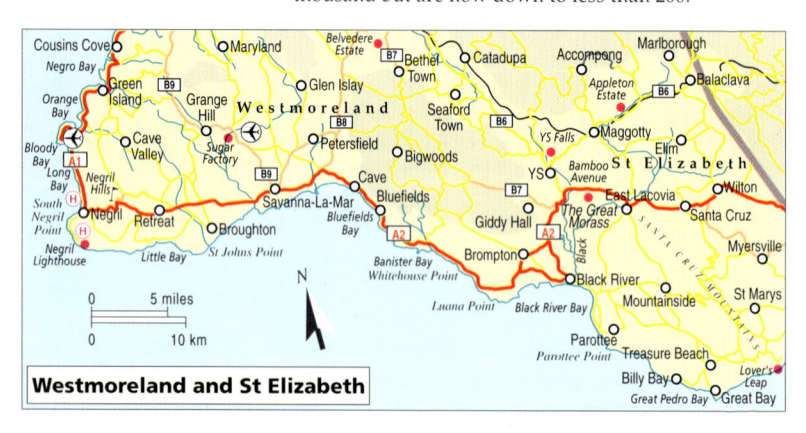

In the grounds of Seaford's **Church of the Sacred Heart**, the **Seaford Town Historical Mini-Museum** traces the sad history of the Seaford Town Germans from their arrival from northern Germany in 1834 to the present day.

ST ELIZABETH PARISH
Black River and the Great Morass ***

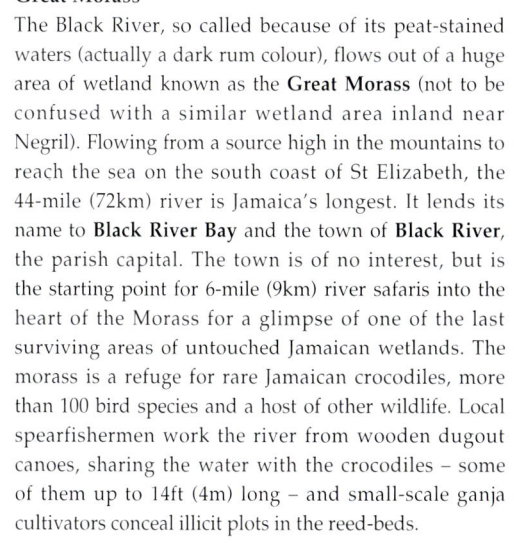

The Black River, so called because of its peat-stained waters (actually a dark rum colour), flows out of a huge area of wetland known as the **Great Morass** (not to be confused with a similar wetland area inland near Negril). Flowing from a source high in the mountains to reach the sea on the south coast of St Elizabeth, the 44-mile (72km) river is Jamaica's longest. It lends its name to **Black River Bay** and the town of **Black River**, the parish capital. The town is of no interest, but is the starting point for 6-mile (9km) river safaris into the heart of the Morass for a glimpse of one of the last surviving areas of untouched Jamaican wetlands. The morass is a refuge for rare Jamaican crocodiles, more than 100 bird species and a host of other wildlife. Local spearfishermen work the river from wooden dugout canoes, sharing the water with the crocodiles – some of them up to 14ft (4m) long – and small-scale ganja cultivators conceal illicit plots in the reed-beds.

YS Falls ***

This 2500-acre (1012ha) farm 8 miles (12km) north of Black River, with thoroughbred racehorses, pedigree Red Poll cattle, and papaya plantations, has been owned by the Browne family since 1887 but was founded by John Yates and Richard Scott in 1684 and takes its name from the initials of its first owners. The main attraction is

Above: *Fishing boats lie moored at the mouth of the Black River.*

CROCODILES

The Jamaican crocodile (often, and incorrectly, called 'alligator') is one of the world's rarest. A glance at the map, with its scattering of placenames like **Alligator Pond** and **Alligator Hole**, is a hint that these leathery leviathans were once much more numerous. The biggest threats to the Jamaican croc today are theft of its eggs, which are sometimes eaten, and more importantly the rapid destruction of its wetland habitats. The best place to see crocodiles is on the **Black River**, which has the largest breeding population on the island and where some crocodiles have become so used to visitors that they can even be touched.

WESTMORELAND AND ST ELIZABETH

a series of cascades on the **YS River**, which tumbles through lush woodland. Visitors are able to swim in the 20 waterfall pools and stroll through paths lined with bamboo, red ginger and scarlet-flowered bird of paradise shrubs. Open 09:30–15:30 Tuesday–Sunday.

Appleton Estate ★★

The distillery and the sugar-cane plantation in the lovely Black River valley attract tours from resorts all over the island, and it is here where visitors may see Jamaica's sugar cane turned into fine rum at the island's biggest distillery, the heart of the **J. Wray and Nephew Ltd** operation since the mid-18th century. Rum is aged in thousands of oak barrels, and the plantation covers more than 4000 acres (1620ha). Open 09:00–15:30 daily.

Accompong ★

There is little to see at Accompong, the main settlement of the **Cockpit Country Maroons**, but the drive – especially the last eight miles (13km) from **Maggotty** – is an adven-

MAROON REBELS

Many Maroons were experienced warriors, sold into slavery by their African enemies after defeat in battle, and none had any reason to love their white masters. Their charismatic leader **Cudjoe** became the greatest of Maroon chiefs. Rather than attempt to confront enemy British troops and island militia in open country – where European firearms put them at a disadvantage – the Maroons chose to fight in the thick forests of the **Cockpit Country** and the **Blue Mountains**. Here their skill in ambush, led by Cudjoe, made them virtually invincible.

Right: *Lush greenery covers a series of cascades on the YS River in St Elizabeth parish; the river takes its name from the initials of the original owners of the surrounding land.*

ture in itself. One look at the steep hillsides and jungle-choked canyons is enough to explain how the Maroons (see p. 13) were able to resist conquest for centuries. And this is the accessible part of the Maroon country – there is no road through the Cockpit Country, north of Accompong.

Above: *From Lovers' Leap on the south coast there are extensive views along the shore and inland.*

Treasure Beach **

Like Bluefields, this tiny, scattered community of farmers and fishermen attracts a scattering of determined escapists who feel Negril has become too commercialised. That is certainly not a charge which could be levelled at Treasure Beach, where two small hotels and a bunch of budget guesthouses, plus two or three simple restaurants, are the only signs of tourism. The beach is not as good as those at Negril or on the north coast – rough sand instead of gleaming white powder – but it is virtually empty of holidaymakers, who find the 20-mile (32km) drive from Black River – and over bad roads – sufficient deterrent. There are no organised watersports, but you are able to charter a fishing boat for a day's fishing and snorkelling or for a trip around **Parottee Point** to Black River.

Lovers' Leap *

The only sightseeing attraction on the south coast, a red-and-white lighthouse perched 1500ft (460m) above the sea, is the landmark for one of the most spectacular viewpoints in Jamaica, with sweeping views of the coast to east and west, and inland to the **Santa Cruz Mountains** which dominate the southern part of St Elizabeth parish. Local legend attributes the name to a suicide love pact between two slaves who threw themselves from the cliff rather than be captured and separated.

DUPPIES

Given the island's bloody history, from the ruthless extermination of the Arawaks through to the slave uprisings, battles between Britons and Spaniards, the buccaneering era and the Maroon wars, it's hardly surprising that many Jamaicans retain a belief in 'duppies' – the spirits of those who have come to a violent end, doomed to walk the night forever. Among them are the ghosts of **Lovers' Leap**, on the St Elizabeth coast, where two slave sweethearts are said to have jumped to their deaths rather than be separated, while Bob Marley's track *Duppy Conqueror* is a celebration of the man who walks unafraid of his fate.

Westmoreland & St Elizabeth at a Glance

BEST TIMES TO VISIT

Jamaica's climate is moderate year-round, but the heat and humidity May–November, along with seasonal rains, make it officially off-season.

GETTING THERE

By **road**, Negril is 52 miles (81km) from Mo Bay on the A1 and 153 miles (240km) from Kingston on the A2. No public road transport, but JUTA (see Useful Contacts) runs shuttle **buses** to Mo Bay. **Air Jamaica** flies to Negril from Montego Bay and Kingston.

GETTING AROUND

24hr-taxis cruise hotels and nightspots in Negril, and there is a taxi rank at Adrija Plaza. Hire **bicycles** and **motorcycles** at hotels and outlets in Negril. Jeep and **car hire** is also available.

WHERE TO STAY

Negril
LUXURY

Beachcomber Club, Norman Manley Boulevard, PO Box 98, Negril, tel: 957 4170, fax: 957 4097. 45 suites, kitchen and large ocean-view verandah.
Charela Inn, Norman Manley Boulevard, PO Box 33, Negril, tel: 957 4277, fax: 957 4414. 40 air-con rooms for families; garden, pool and watersports.
Grand Lido, PO Box 88, Negril, tel: 957 5010, fax: 957 5517. Super-inclusive on Bloody Bay; excellent restaurants, and all the luxuries. No tipping.

Negril Inn, PO Box 59, Negril, tel: 957 4209, fax: 957 4385. All-inclusive, private balconies or patios, restaurant, bars, disco, and sports.
Poinciana Beach Resort, Norman Manley Boulevard, Negril PO, tel: 957 5100, fax: 957 5229. All-inclusive villas and suites with superior service.
Point Village Resort, Norman Manley Boulevard, PO Box 105, Negril, tel: 957 5170, fax: 957 4351. One-, two-, or three-bedroom suites in all-inclusive on the Point Rutland Peninsula; landscaped grounds; private beaches; family facilities. Superb value for money.
Sandals Negril, Norman Manley Boulevard, PO Box 12, Negril, tel: 957 5216, fax: 957 5338. Couples-only all-inclusive on private section of Negril Beach, restaurants and bars.
Swept Away Resort, Norman Manley Boulevard, PO Box 77, Negril, tel: 957 4061, fax: 957 4060. Couples-only all-inclusive, 10 acres (4ha) of sport facilities, 20 acres (8ha) of landscaped grounds; restaurants and bars.

MID-RANGE

Hedonism II, Norman Manley Boulevard, PO Box 25, Negril, tel: 957 5200, fax: 957 5289. All-inclusive for party animals; sports, buffet, nude beach, bar, disco, and circus workshop.
Negril Cabins Resort, Norman Manley Boulevard, PO Box 118, Negril, tel: 957 4350, fax: 957 4381. Timber cottages in tropical garden.

Negril Gardens Hotel, Norman Manley Boulevard, PO Box 58, Negril, tel: 957 4408, fax: 957 4374. Comfortable, attractive gardens on beach.
Our Past Time Hotel, Norman Manley Boulevard, PO Box 45, Negril, tel: 957 5931 (no fax). Beachfront, restaurant, bar; facilities for children.

BUDGET

Addis Kokeb, West End, PO Box 78, Negril, tel/fax: 957 4485. Nine rooms and cottages, kitchen, hammocks. Babysitting service, and sea access.
Heartbeat Cottage, West End Road, PO Box 95, Negril, tel: 957 4329, fax: 957 0069. Good value cottages overlooking the West End cliffs.
Xtabi Resort, West End Road, PO Box 19, Negril, tel: 957 4336, fax: 957 0121. Wooden cottages with view. No beach.

Black River
MID-RANGE

Ashton Great House and Hotel, PO Box 104, Luana, Black River, tel/fax: 965 2036. Fine views, 4 miles (7km) north of Black River on A2.
Invercauld Great House and Hotel, High Street, PO Box 12, Black River, tel: 965 2750, fax: 965 2751. Period furnishings, on the Black River waterfront.

BUDGET

Bridge House Inn, 14 Crane Road, Black River, tel: 965 2361 (no fax). Small, basic, family-run guesthouse.

Westmoreland & St Elizabeth at a Glance

Bluefields
MID-RANGE
Bluefields Bay Villas, Bluefields, Westmoreland, tel: 997 5043, fax: 995 9080. Bungalows may be rented by the week on Bluefields beach.
Shafston Estate Great House, Bluefields PO, Westmoreland, tel: 997 5076 (no fax). Comfortable, very affordable; restored in 1992.

Treasure Beach
LUXURY
Sunset Resort Villas, Calabash Bay, Treasure Beach, tel: 965 0143, fax: 965 0555. Comfortable, family-run hotel overlooking the beach.
Treasure Beach Hotel, Treasure Beach, PO Box 5, Black River, tel: 965 2305, fax: 965 0114. Comfortable 36 ocean-front rooms and suites, swimming pool and restaurant.

MID-RANGE
Jake's Village, Calabash Bay, Treasure Beach, St Elizabeth, tel/fax: 965 0552. Unique and colourful guesthouse, excellent restaurant and miniature beach; excellent value.
Olde Wharf Resort, Callabash Bay, Treasure Beach, St Elizabeth, tel: 965 0110, fax: 965 2544. Simple, modest rooms, some sport facilities.

BUDGET
Four M Cottage, PO Box 4, Mountainside, Treasure Beach, tel: 965 0131. Affordable guesthouse, camping sites.

WHERE TO EAT
Most of the restaurants in Negril have a happy hour at sunset, while many others offer all-you-can-eat buffets. Elsewhere in Westmoreland and St Elizabeth, dining choices are rather limited.

Negril
LUXURY
Kuyaba Beach Restaurant and Bar, Norman Manley Boulevard, tel 957 4318. Fine food throughout the day and in the evening in stunning exotic surroundings on the beach. Free pick up from your hotel.
Tan Ya's, Seasplash Resort, Norman Manley Boulevard, Negril, tel: 957 4041. European and classical cuisine combined with new Jamaican influences. Open-air dining.
La Vendome, Charela Inn (see *Where to Stay*), tel: 957 4277. Open-air fine dining, French and Jamaican cuisine, excellent wine list, live music.

MID-RANGE
Country Country Bar & Grill, Norman Manley Boulevard, Negril, tel: 957 4273. Newly renovated beach restaurant seving seafood, vegetarian, and Chinese dishes.
Alfred's Ocean Palace, PO Box 3081, Negril, tel: 957 4669 or 957 4735, fax: 957 9674. Family owned and operated seaside restaurant and bar in the heart of Negril, specialising in locally caught lobster, conch, mahi mahi, tuna, kingfish and calamari. Dine in the dining room or at a candle lit table under the stars. Menu changes frequently.

TOURS AND EXCURSIONS
Negril Scuba Centre, Negril Beach Club, tel: 957 4425. Dive training, scuba resort courses, dive trips and also night dives.
Ocean Tours Water Sports, Fisherman's Club, Negril Beach, tel: 957 4693. Reef tours, cave cruises, Booby Cay island picnics, sunset cruises, fishing and snorkelling trips, waterskiing, banana boat rides, jet ski rental and parascending.
Anancy Fun Park, located at Poinciana Beach Resort, open daily, tel: 957 5100. Fun attraction for kids with water slides and games, themed around Jamaica's folk tale character, Anancy the spider.

USEFUL CONTACTS
Jamaica Tourist Board, Coral Seas Plaza, Negril, tel: 957 4243.
Jamaica Tourist Board, 2 High Street, Black River, tel: 965 2074.
JUTA (main Negril Office), Negril Community Centre, tel: 957 9197 (beach office); Norman Manley Boulevard, tel: 957 3117.
Easy Going Cabs, West End Road, Negril, tel: 957 3227. Airport shuttle, local journeys, 24hr service.

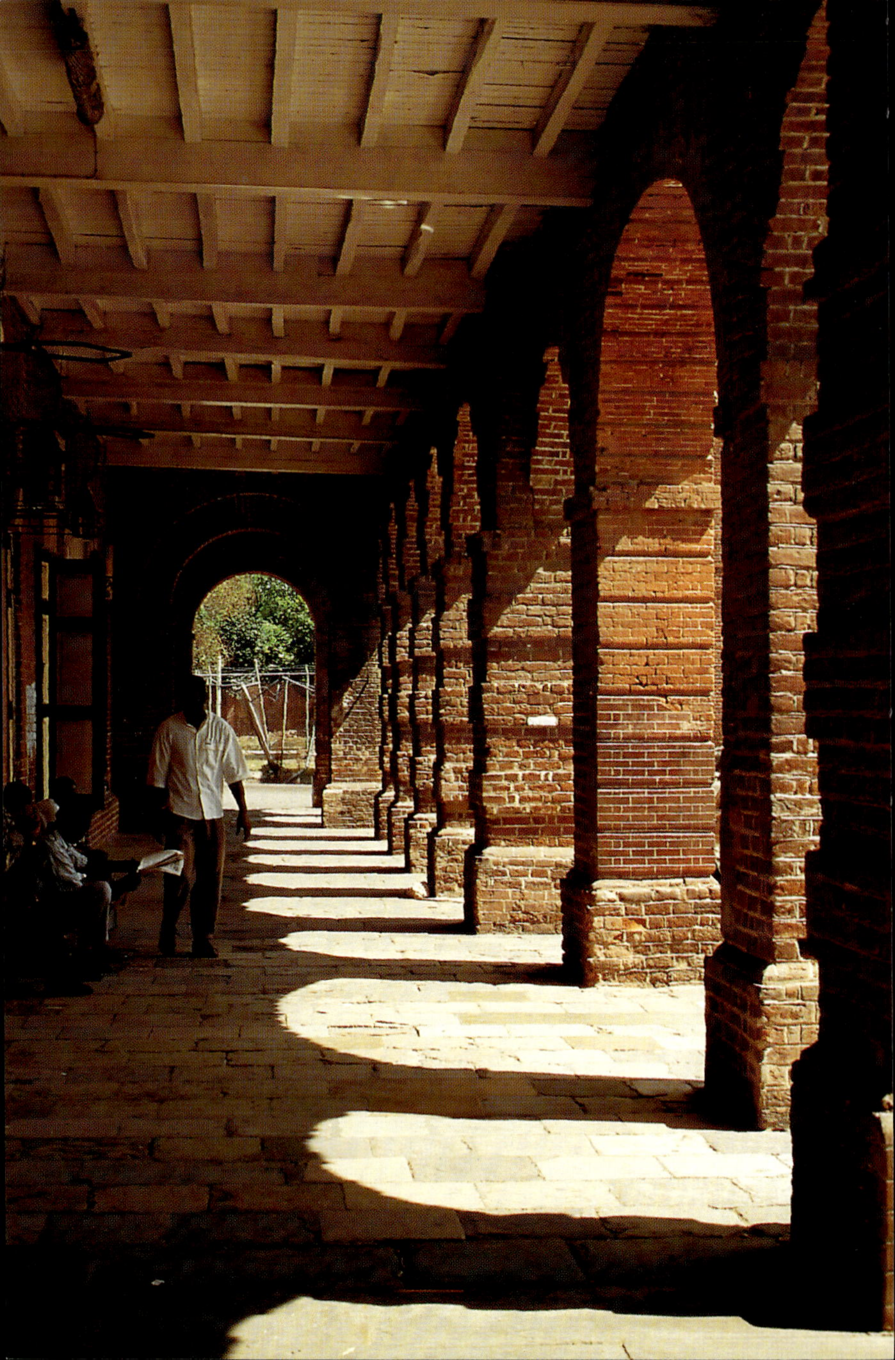

7
Manchester, Clarendon and St Catherine

The parishes of Middlesex are the island's most populous, with three large farming and commercial towns, but the south coast west of Kingston sees fewer tourists than any other part of the Jamaica – because it has fewer outstanding beaches and few decent roads. The A2 route runs east and inland through **Manchester** and **Clarendon**, leaving the south shore intriguingly hard to get to. Though rich in history – **Spanish Town** was Jamaica's first sizeable settlement and its seat of government until Kingston became the capital – the three parishes are not over-endowed with natural or manmade attractions, and for most visitors to the island they are points to pass through en route between brighter, busier resorts.

Nevertheless, they are places where you can see a side of Jamaica very different from the resorts and sightseeing experiences offered by the commercialised north shore. In the villages and towns of the south people live a lifestyle largely immune from the impact of multi-million-dollar tourism and the fast-paced, fast-changing fashions of Kingston. This is largely farming country, with cattle ranches and citrus, spice and coffee plantations, while the fishing settlements dotted around the coast show little sign of being transformed into holiday resorts. If you have a rugged enough vehicle and are prepared to brave the poorly surfaced and mostly signpost-free roads leading to the south coast, you'll find the last stretches of undeveloped shoreline in Jamaica. Alternatively, if you venture into the hills above **Mandeville** you will be rewarded with cool breezes and outstanding views.

CARIBBEAN SEA

Don't Miss

*** **Cathedral of St Jago de la Vega:** Jamaica's most beautiful church.
** **White Marl Arawak Museum:** recreation of Arawak life.
** **Hellshire Beaches:** the best and busiest resorts.
** **Williamsfield Great House:** restored plantation manor-house.
** **High Mountain Coffee Factory:** see coffee being processed from the field.
* **Marshall's Pen Great House:** historic home on a working estate; great for birdwatching.

Opposite: *The cloistered arcades of the old Records Office in Spanish Town.*

BAUXITE

The red dust which coats the landscape near **Ocho Rios** and **Mandeville** is bauxite – **aluminium ore** – which, apart from tourism, sugar and ganja, is one of Jamaica's main sources of foreign currency. Bauxite mining is open-cast, resulting in severe scarring of the landscape, but the industry is a major employer and Jamaica is the world's biggest producer of the mineral. Biggest of the foreign companies which mine more than 10 million tons of Jamaican bauxite is **Alcan**, and its huge **Kirkvine Works** outside Mandeville can be visited by the public.

MANDEVILLE AND SURROUNDS
Mandeville **

High among the **Don Figuerero Mountains** (named after one of the Spanish conquistadors), Mandeville has a cooler climate than the coast, thanks to an elevation of almost 2100ft (630m). The average local temperatures are around 3C° (6F°) cooler than at sea level, with daytime temperatures no higher than 27°C (80°F). This has always made it a popular getaway spot for wealthier Kingstonians, who visit to play a round of golf at the **Manchester Club** or go riding in the surrounding hills, and has led to the description of the town as 'more English than England' – presumably by someone who never set foot outside Jamaica. There's nothing English about Mandeville – not even the climate, which is far more pleasant than anything the UK has to offer. North of town the scenery is a little marred by the largest open-cast bauxite mine in the world and an alumina processing mill.

Only 57 miles (89km) from Kingston on the A1, Mandeville is even attracting middle-class Jamaicans away from the heat and stress of the city, and many new residential homes have been built on the outskirts of town. Coffee and spices grow well in the hill country around Mandeville, and among the town sights are two factories producing some of Jamaica's best known export delicacies – fine coffee and piquant sauces and pickles.

Above: *Mandeville's comparatively cool climate made it a popular refuge for affluent Kingstonians in previous centuries, who settled here in numbers and built opulent homes in the surrounding hill country.*

Williamsfield Great House **

North of the town centre, Williamsfield Great House is an immaculately restored example of the plantation manor, built in 1770 by **Captain George Heron**, one of the biggest landowners in Manchester parish, where he lorded it over a 10,000-acre (4047ha) estate. Inside, paintings, furniture and decorations reflect the grandeur of the 18th-century sugar planter's way of life. Tours by arrangement only.

High Mountain Coffee Factory **

Also at Williamsfield, visitors may watch coffee being processed – from treating the green berries through the roasting and grinding process to sealing and packaging. The tours, by appointment only, provide a fascinating insight into an everyday commodity.

Pickapeppa Factory **

Just a little further north of Williamsfield, at **Shooter's Hill**, the Pickapeppa Factory will appeal to anyone with a taste for spicy sauces. Pickapeppa makes a range of delicious pickles, flavourings and sauces from the many different tropical spices growing in Jamaica, but the exact recipe is kept top secret. Tours of the factory and plantations are by arrangement only.

MANDEVILLE COCKTAIL

- 2 measures dark rum
- Half measure lemon juice
- 1 teaspoon Pernod
- Quarter teaspoon of grenadine
- Top up with Coca-Cola. Shake ingredients thoroughly with ice and pour into a tumbler. Top again with Coke and add an orange slice for decoration.

Marshall's Pen Great House **

Around 2½ miles (4km) northwest of the town centre, at **Hibiscus Gardens**, Marshall's Pen Great House is still the headquarters of a working cattle estate. Its extensive woods and fields are a refuge for many Jamaican bird species, some of them rare, and owner Robert Sutton is a renowned expert on Jamaican birds. Tours of the house and grounds are by prior arrangement only.

Christiana *

This small town 13 miles (21km) north of Mandeville is 2900ft (950m) above sea level and set among cool, green surroundings. The scenery is well worth the 20-minute drive and, if you are touring the island by car, Christiana is an ideal place to spend a night. With its panoramic views, Christiana boasts one of the most pleasant small hotels in Jamaica.

Right: *One of the plantation houses around Mandeville, Marshall's Pen Great House, is still the centre of a working cattle estate; splendid wooden beams line the interior of the house.*

SOUTH COAST
Long Bay

Head west from **Milk River**, past the rather scruffy fishing settlement of **Farquhar's Beach** and you will come upon the last long stretch of undeveloped beach in Jamaica – a 15-mile (24km) sweep of coastline which looks much as it must have done before the Spaniards arrived. An unsurfaced and deeply pot-holed track follows the coastline along Long Bay to picturesque **Old Woman's Point** and on to **Alligator Pond**, a fishing village which has the only accommodation on this stretch of coast.

Milk River Bath *

On the south coast of **Clarendon** parish, 18 miles (28km) south of **May Pen**, Milk River Bath's claim to fame is its radioactive thermal spring, claimed to alleviate aches, pains and skin infections. The spring's healing properties are said to have been discovered by a slave who had been beaten almost to death (a similar story is told about the spa at Bath, in St Thomas parish, *see p. 56*) and whose wounds were healed by immersion in the hot waters. The public baths and thermal swimming pool of **Milk River Spa** are open 10:00–18:00 weekends and public holidays.

May Pen

May Pen is a small commercial and farming town in the heart of Clarendon parish, 20 miles (32km) west of Spanish Town and set among some of Jamaica's richest agricultural land. The Denbigh Agricultural and Industrial Show, the biggest event of the year for Jamaica's farmers, is held at May Pen every August.

Halse Hall *

Built in the 17th century by **Thomas Halse**, who was one of the earliest British settlers, Halse Hall is a gracious building in limestone with wooden balconies and verandas. Recent restoration has returned much of its former grandeur, and it is beautifully furnished with colonial antiques. Open to visitors by prior arrangement only.

RASTAFARI

Born in the 1930s, Rastafarianism is a melange of Old Testament Christianity, back-to-Africa fundamentalism and ganja-fuelled mysticism. It identifies African-Caribbean people with the enslaved **Israelites**, and white culture with **Babylon**. **Haile Selassie**, Emperor of Ethiopia, (one of whose titles was **Ras Tafari**, meaning 'lion prince') was venerated by Rastas as a living god. Ruler of the only African nation free of white rulers, he was a potent symbol of black pride. Real Rastas try to live in self-sufficient communities independent of 'Babylon' (one such group still struggles along in Ethiopia, 30 years after its foundation on land granted by Haile Selassie), but there are plenty whose commitment goes no deeper than growing the mandatory, matted 'dreadlocks' and smoking ganja, regarded by true Rastas as a sacrament.

CHRISTOPHER COLUMBUS

Why do we still call the Caribbean the **West Indies** and its people **West Indians**? It's all due to Christopher Columbus. Born around 1450, Columbus went to sea aged 14, and became captain of his own ships trading between the Mediterranean and the Atlantic islands. Convinced that sailing westward would bring him to **Asia**, he persuaded **King Ferdinand** and **Queen Isabella** of **Spain** to finance his voyages of exploration. His second expedition, in 1493, brought him to Jamaica. Over the next decade he explored the Caribbean, while insisting that this was in fact Asia – 'the Indies'. In 1503, his ships returned to Jamaica after an arduous voyage from Darien (Panama) and spent almost a year making repairs. He eventually returned to Spain, where he died in May 1506.

Colbeck Castle *

Just outside the village of **Old Harbour**, 13 miles (20km) west of Spanish Town, and once one of the most imposing of Jamaica's mansion houses, Colbeck Castle is now a ruin standing among sugar cane and tobacco fields. Its builder, **Colonel John Colbeck**, is said to have been one of the first English settlers. Features which can still be seen include the slave dungeons adjoining the house.

SPANISH TOWN

Spanish Town, 14 miles (23km) west of Kingston on the A1 highway, appears at first to be an unprepossessing sprawl of modern low-rise concrete buildings. But Spanish Town is more than just a residential satellite of the capital. In 1523 its ideal location close to Kingston's natural harbour lured Spanish colonists away from their first settlement, which was unhealthily located near fever swamps at Sevilla la Nueva on the north coast. They called the new settlement Villa de la Vega (City of the Plain).

The Spaniards were not the first to see the advantages of what is now Spanish Town, for before they arrived this had been the site of the island's largest **Arawak** village. Nor were they the last – Cromwell's troops sacked the city in 1655 and built a new town on the ruins, which remained the seat of government until 1872. Relics of Spanish Town's heyday include the buildings around the square which rank among the region's finest surviving examples of 18th-century architecture. Built to show the wealth of the sugar industry, **Old Assembly House** (now the **Parish Council Building**) dominates the square's east side, with long brick arcades and wooden balconies. Like the **King's House**, on the opposite side of the square, it was built in 1762.

Rodney Memorial *

At the north end of the **Parade** – originally the central plaza of Villa de la Vega – stands the startlingly elegant Rodney Memorial, with its classic white marble colonnades and porticos. A toga-draped statue of **Admiral George Rodney**, a near-contemporary of Admiral Nelson, stands in front of the building, sheltered by a six-sided cupola. Rodney's fleet trounced a Spanish and French armada off Jamaica in 1782.

Spanish Town Archaeological Museum *

The King's House, on the Parade, was built in 1762 and served as the town residence of the royal representative in Jamaica, the Governor, until the seat of government moved to Kingston. In 1925 it was partially destroyed in a fire, but its stylish Georgian portico and frontage have survived, while the reconstructed building within now houses a small collection of artefacts from the Spanish Town site, including Spanish doubloons, weapons and tools. Open 10:00–16:00 Monday–Friday.

Jamaican People's Museum of Craft and Technology *

Also on the Parade and alongside the King's House is the **Jamaican People's Museum of Craft and Technology**. This collection, housed in what was once the Governor's stables, includes exhibits of everyday tools, utensils and other bygones, including a recreation of a village store complete with stock. Open 10:00–16:00 Monday–Friday.

Cathedral of St Jago de la Vega *

Built in 1714, the cathedral stands on the Parade on the site of a 16th-century Spanish church of St Jago (St James) which was destroyed by the British invaders when they seized the town in 1655. With its carved wooden pews and interior columns, ceiling beams and colourful stained glass windows, it is considered by many as Jamaica's most beautiful church.

Above: *Admiral Rodney's fleet kept Jamaica from French invasion during the 18th century.*
Opposite: *Colbeck Castle was named after an early English settler who arrived in Jamaica with Oliver Cromwell's army in 1655.*

18TH-CENTURY WEALTH

By the mid-18th century there were more than 400 vast **sugar estates** on the island, each a self-sufficient entity. From his lavish, stone-built mansion, the planter (estate owner) was lord of all he surveyed, from the streets of slave barracks to the stables, the small houses of European clerks and overseers, the smoky buildings of the sugar mill and refining works, and the rolling green-gold sea of canefields.

SUNBURN

Caribbean skies can be cloudy, but there is always the risk of burning, especially for those with fair skins. On a catamaran or sailboard, the spray and the cool breeze disguise the strength of the sun and it is all too easy to burn. It's even easier to overdo it while snorkelling, when your back and shoulders are exposed while the rest of your body is below water. Use **sunscreen** on sensitive areas such as lips, ears and nose, and high-factor sunscreen or, even better, wear a T-shirt when sailing or snorkelling. Locally made **aloe gel** is an excellent soother for scorched skin.

Below: *The White Marl Museum contains a range of Arawak artefacts, some reconstructed on the basis of surviving evidence.*

White Marl Arawak Museum *

This museum stands on the site of the island's largest Arawak village, 3 miles (5km) east of the town centre on the A1 highway. The village has been recreated with an exhibition of Arawak tools, weapons and utensils, and information on their long-lost way of life, reconstructed by archaeologists from the evidence found in the remnants of their settlement. Open 10:00–16:00 Monday–Friday.

PORTMORE

Portmore's population has soared from around 80,000 to 150,000 since the 1980s. A 3-mile (5km) road causeway across **Kingston Harbour** connects the small residential town with the capital. South of the town lie the **Hellshire Hills**. This area of arid scrubland shelters a variety of rare species indigenous to Jamaica – including the Jamaican iguana and the rabbit-like Jamaican coney – but is gradually disappearing under a tide of new residential building. The southwest shore of the Hellshire peninsula is covered by muddy mangrove swamps which remain more attractive to the rare manatee than to the tourism industry. Nevertheless, the beaches of the east coast, close to Kingston, attract droves of city-dwellers every weekend. Portmore's other claim to fame is **Caymanas Park**, Jamaica's biggest racetrack. Racing takes place here every Wednesday and Saturday and on public holidays.

Hellshire Beaches **

On the east coast of the Hellshire peninsula, about three miles (5km) south of Portmore and across the bay from Kingston, a string of sandy beaches attract thousands of Kingstonians at weekends and on public holidays. For beach life Jamaican-style, head for **Fort Clarence Beach**, where there are frequent beauty shows, muscle contests, live music, beach games, barbecues, and food shacks selling fish, lobster and jerk meat. **Naggo Heads**, just north of Fort Clarence and separated from Portmore by the lagoon called the **Great Salt Pond**, is even more popular with local Jamaicans.

Manchester, Clarendon & St Catherine at a Glance

Best Times to Visit

Jamaica's climate is moderate year-round, but the heat and humidity May–November, along with seasonal rains, make it officially off-season.

Getting There

A2 highway runs west from Negril through Savanna Mar and Black River, into Middlesex, connecting Mandeville with May Pen and Spanish Town. The **A1 highway** connects Kingston with Spanish Town, Portmore, and the north coast.

Getting Around

Off the highways, **roads** are poorly surfaced and erratically signposted. **Taxis** are best, but agree on a price in advance.

Where to Stay

There are few hotels in Middlesex as most visitors just pass through. No recommended accommodation in Spanish Town, Portmore or May Pen.

Mandeville
Mid-range

Astra Country Inn, 62 Ward Avenue, Mandeville, tel: 962 3725, fax: 962 1461. 22 rooms, off-the-beach vacation. Good Jamaican restaurant.
Mandeville Hotel, 4 Hotel Street, Mandeville, tel: 962 2138, fax: 962 0700. 60 rooms; central, golf, tennis, coffee shop, pool, restaurants, bars.
Golf View Hotel, 51–2 Caledonia Avenue, Mandeville, Manchester, tel: 962 4471/7, fax: 962 5640. Modern, 45 room, overlooking golf course.

Budget

Kariba Kariba Guesthouse, 39 New Green Road, PO Box 482, Mandeville, Jamaica, tel: 962 8006, fax: 962 5502. Accessible; spacious rooms, in orange and grapefruit groves.

Alligator Pond
Mid-range

Sea Rivers Inn, Bull Savannah, Alligator Pond, Manchester, tel: 962 7265 (no fax). Seaside hotel, on an undeveloped beach.

Christiana
Mid-range

Hotel Villa Bella, Christiana, Manchester, tel: 964 2243, fax: 964 2765. Atmospheric, 18-room inn; excellent restaurant.

Where to Eat

Mandeville has a selection of restaurants, but other food and drink options are in the few hotels, fast-food outlets and basic food shacks (Rasta fishermen at Farquhar's Beach, near Milk River, will cook fresh seafood with Jamaican trimmings).

Mandeville
Luxury

Bill Laurie's, Bloomfield Gardens, Mandeville, tel: 962 3116. Steak and grill restaurant with superb views; the establishment doubles as an antique car museum.

Mid-range

Astra Country Inn, (see Where to Stay). Award-winning restaurant, Jamaican and European cuisine.

Tours and Excursions

Countryside Tours, based at the Astra Country Inn (see Where to Stay), has pioneered 'community-based tourism' with excursions throughout the region. Walking and riding in the Clarendon hills can also be arranged through the **Hotel Villa Bella** (see Where to Stay).
Kariba Leisure Tours, PO Box 482, Mandeville, tel: 962 8006, fax: 962 5502. Off-the-beaten-track excursions to Black River, Bamboo Avenue, Appleton Estate and the south coast.
Williamsfield Great House, tel: 963 4214. Tours by prior arrangement.
High Mountain Coffee Factory, tel: 963 4211. Tours by appointment only.
Pickapeppa Factory, tel: 962 2928. Tours of the factory and plantations by arrangement.
Marshall's Pen Great House, tel: 963 8569. Tours of house and grounds by arrangement only.
Halse Hall, tel: 986 2215. Open to visitors by arrangement only.

Useful Contacts

Jamaica Tourist Board, 11 Ward Avenue, tel: 962 1072.

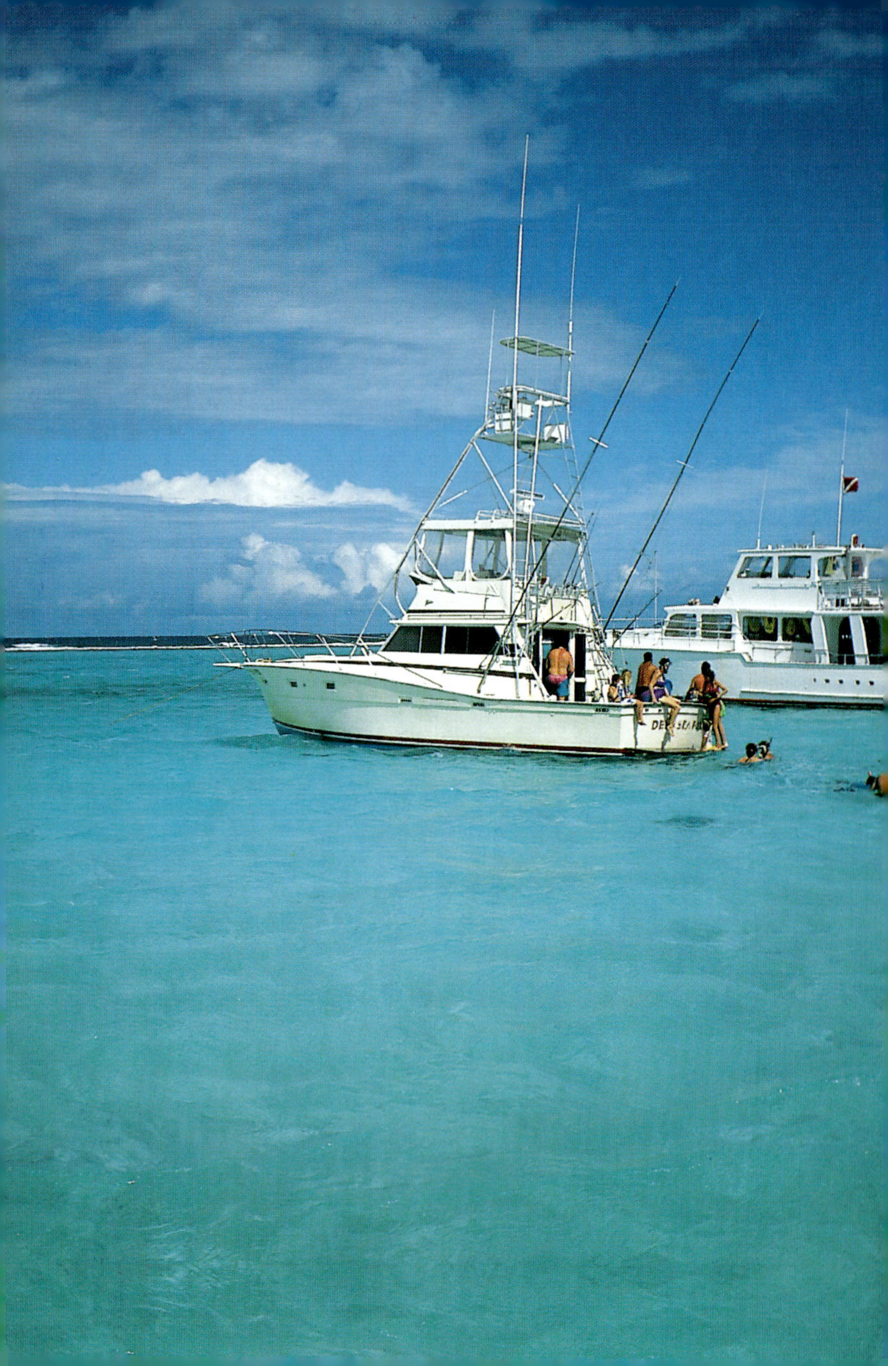

8
The Cayman Islands

The Cayman Islands could hardly present a greater contrast to Jamaica, less than an hour's flying time away. Jamaica is one of the Caribbean's biggest, most populous islands. Cayman (only visitors to this Caribbean microstate call it by its full name) comprises three tiny isles – the largest only 28 miles (44km) long and 7 miles (12km) wide. The archipelago has a population of only 30,000 multi-racial descendants of Cromwellian deserters, Spanish refugees, castaways and buccaneers who began settling the then uninhabited islands around 1670, some 167 years after their discovery by **Christopher Columbus**. Cayman resorts are at once quieter, more relaxed and more upmarket than Jamaica's upbeat beaches, and its people are much more reserved than their outgoing Caribbean neighbours.

The Cayman Islands has become one of the region's wealthier economies, thanks to extremely liberal banking and financial regulations that have attracted financiers and money manipulators from all over the world. This once sleepy nation of farmer-fishermen is now one of the world's most respected and sought-after financial centres. Cool sea breezes make the Cayman climate easier to deal with than the heat of the Jamaican coast, another bonus for its business visitors. Cayman's top attractions are both above and below the waterline – there are beaches to rival any in the Caribbean, an excellent golf course, island hideaways on the smaller isles and top-quality watersports, including diving.

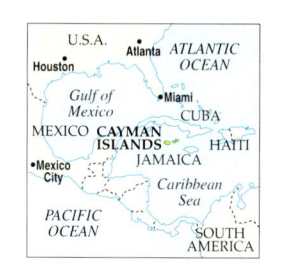

Don't Miss

*** **Stingray City:** snorkel with dozens of harmless, friendly giant rays.
*** **Seven Mile Beach:** powder white sand with great hotels and watersports.
** **Mastic Trail:** explore the Cayman wilderness.
** **Turtle Farm:** see hundreds of giant green turtles, hatched in captivity for release into the wild.
*** **Scuba diving:** hundreds of fantastic dive sites on all three islands.

Opposite: *Boats anchor over Stingray City at Grand Cayman.*

> **CAYMAN HISTORY**
>
> **1503** Christopher Columbus sights the Caymans on his fourth voyage, naming them 'Las Tortugas' (the turtles) because of the huge numbers of green turtles in the surrounding waters.
> **1585** Sir Francis Drake's fleet anchors off Grand Cayman.
> **1668** Settlers from Jamaica are driven out of Little Cayman and Cayman Brac by Spanish pirates.
> **1670** Caymans become British by Treaty of Madrid.
> **1734** First settlers granted land in the Caymans.
> **1833** First permanent settlers move to Cayman Brac.

Underwater Cayman

It is below the surface that Cayman really shines, for this is one of the world's great diving destinations, with visibility of up to 200ft (60m) and abundant reef life for both shallow and deep divers. The three islands have too many perfect dive sites to list, with more than 150 shallow dives, wrecks and wall dives scattered around **Grand Cayman** alone. Grand Cayman is noted for its walls, some sloping gently, others plummeting into one of the world's deepest trenches. Wrecks off Grand Cayman include the *Doc Polson*, the *Oro Verde*, the *Balboa* and the LCM *David Nicholson*, all off the **West Side** of the island, and the *Ridgefield*, off the **East End**. Cayman Brac has the newest wreck in Cayman waters – the 330ft (100m) former Soviet warship *#356*. Cayman Brac also has wall dives and miles of shallow reefs, and **Bloody Bay Wall**, the best known of Little Cayman's dives, is a 1200ft (390m) vertical plunge which is rated one of the world's top dive sites.

GRAND CAYMAN

Grand Cayman is shaped like a whale swimming from west to east, with **Seven Mile Beach** running along the outer edge of its tail flipper and **George Town**, the island capital, at the base of the tail. **Rum Point**, midway along the north coast, forms the dorsal fin. The biggest and most populous of the three islands – with more than double the land area of the others – it is home to 26,000 islanders,

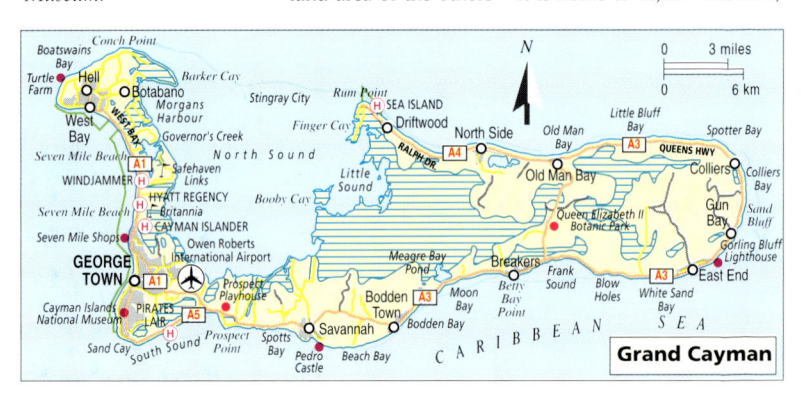

Opposite: *Prosperous George Town, the capital of the Cayman Islands, is the location of the National Museum.*

some of them still fishermen and sailors, but many now involved in one of the two boom businesses which have put this tiny speck on the modern map of the Caribbean: banking and tourism. Its biggest beach is one of the finest in the Caribbean and thanks to a little ingenuity (including the invention of a special short-range golf ball), it has also become a golf destination.

George Town *

The Cayman capital, close to the south end of **Seven Mile Beach**, is mixture of old and new, with gleaming new international banks and duty-free shopping centres ousting older wooden buildings. Signs of the prosperity brought by tourism and international finance are everywhere, and the capital has a surprising choice of restaurants. George Town is a duty-free port, with some outstanding shopping bargains. Also worth a visit is the **Cayman Islands National Museum** on Harbour Drive, which recreates a vanishing way of life, recording the days when Caymanians lived by seafaring. Open 09:00–17:00 Monday–Saturday.

Britannia at Hyatt Golf Course ***

Based at the **Hyatt Regency Hotel** on West Bay Road, Seven Mile Beach, the island's first golf course can be played as a nine-hole championship course, an 18-hole executive course, or an 18-hole Cayman ball course. In the early days of Cayman golf, players found that a ball hit just a touch too hard sank beneath the deep Caribbean which virtually surrounds the course. The solution was the Cayman ball, which flies true but has only half the range of an ordinary golf ball. Open daily, daylight hours.

FACT FILE

Geography: Grand Cayman is 20 miles (32km) long, 4–7 miles (6–11km) wide, and no more than 60ft (18m) above sea level. Little Cayman is 9 miles (14.5km) long and one mile (1.5km) wide, and Cayman Brac 10 miles (16km) long and one mile (1.5km) wide.

Government: British crown colony, governed by a legislative assembly and an executive council of 15 elected members and three members appointed by the governor, who is the Queen's representative.

Population: 32,000 in total, with around 2000 on Little Cayman and only 40 permanent residents on Little Cayman.

Above: *Whether scuba diving or snorkelling, you are guaranteed colourful sights such as this giant anemone in the waters off the Cayman Islands.*

> **SAVING THE TURTLES**
>
> The **green turtles** which once filled Cayman waters in huge numbers were almost wiped out by excessive hunting over three centuries, but in 1971 the **Cayman Turtle Farm** was set up to study and hopefully boost the dwindling numbers. Thousands of eggs are rescued from Cayman beaches each year, and the hatchlings are raised in captivity for later release, increasing the percentage of hatchlings which survive to maturity. Around 30,000 farmed turtles have been tagged and released into the wild. Several thousand turtles each year are also raised for their meat, which is popular with Caymanians but cannot be exported.

Seven Mile Beach ***

This must be one of the world's finest beaches. Running from just north of **George Town** to **North West Point**, Seven Mile Beach has powder white sand, transparent waters, and watersports including world-class diving, windsurfing, parasailing, jet skiing, dinghy sailing and snorkelling among its many attractions.

Safehaven Links Golf Course ***

Another of Cayman's golfing greens is on the West Bay Road at Seven Mile Beach. This 18-hole, par 71 course has established the Cayman Islands as a world-class golfing destination, and attracts a number of golfing enthusiasts to its impressive facilities. Open daily, daylight hours.

Stingray City ***

In only 12ft (4m) of clear water in the **North Sound**, this must surely be the best of the world's shallow-water dive sites, accessible to both snorkellers and complete novices as well as experienced scuba divers. Dozens of stingrays lurk on the bottom of the North Sound. Gentle and harmless, these creatures are accustomed to being fed by divers and will take titbits of squid or fish from your fingers.

Queen Elizabeth II Botanic Park *

Opened by Queen Elizabeth II in 1994, this award-winning 60-acre (24ha) park on Frank Sound Road was established to conserve more than 200 endangered trees and plants, from ironwood and thatch palm to superb orchids – go in May or June to see the best display – as well as birds, including the Grand Cayman parrot and the West Indian woodpecker, and reptiles such as the Grand Cayman blue iguana and the blue-throated Cayman anole lizard. Open 08:30–17:00 Monday-Saturday.

Also within the Botanic Park is the outstanding **Mastic Trail**. Plunge into the bush on a guided tour of the last remaining Grand Cayman wilderness, with the chance to see rare parrots, ajouti, land crabs, iguanas and hundreds of rare flowers, shrubs and trees. Guided tours are conducted at 08:30 daily.

Cayman Islands Turtle Farm *
Once so numerous that Spanish mariners knew the Caymans as **Las Tortugas** (Turtle Islands), the green turtles of the Caribbean have dwindled in numbers. The turtle farm on West Bay aims to boost their numbers in the wild with a breeding and release programme. Thousands of turtles are hatched and raised on the farm each year for release into the ocean for meat. Open 09:00–17:00 daily.

CAYMAN BRAC

Compared with low-lying Grand Cayman, the Brac, 90 miles (145km) to the west, is truly mountainous. The island is some 12 miles (20km) long and no more than one mile (1.8km) wide. The ridge which forms its backbone soars to 140ft (42m) above sea level and is riddled with caves which are said to have been used to hide pirates and their treasure. Many of the islanders are employed in the fishing industry or as merchant seamen, making their homes in **Stake Bay**, the village on the north coast which is the nearest thing Cayman Brac has to a capital.

Above: *Heavenly Seven Mile Beach runs almost the length of the west end of Grand Cayman.*

BLACK CORAL

You will see stores advertising black coral jewellery in **George Town** and other parts of **Grand Cayman**. Found at many depths, the best black coral is found below the 100ft (30m) level and grows slowly – about 1/3 inch (7mm) a year. In 1978, the Islands banned the removal of live black coral from Cayman reefs, but it is now imported from **Belize** and **Honduras**. This smacks of hypocrisy and you are advised not to buy any.

THE CAYMAN ISLANDS

Cut off from the world until the 1960s, 'the Brac' now has an airport which can handle international jets and daily flights from Miami, its own schools and hospital. Young men increasingly head for the bright lights of Grand Cayman or Miami instead of working at sea, and beachfront building lots sell for $50 per square metre or more. That said, Cayman Brac remains a pious and conservative society, with no fewer than 14 churches scattered around the island for a population of 1400 people. Almost all settlement is around the coast, while the interior of the island is a mass of low tropical scrub growing from jagged limestone rock.

Above: *Although Cayman Brac's shoreline is predominantly rocky, there is a small sandy beach in the southwest of the island.*

Russian Destroyer ★★

Purchased from the Russian Navy as scrap and deliberately sunk off the West End as a dive attraction, this wreck is the only diveable Soviet warship in Western waters. The ship was scuttled in 10–60ft (3–20m) of water in September 1996, and the wreck, colonised by marine flora and fauna, offers great diving.

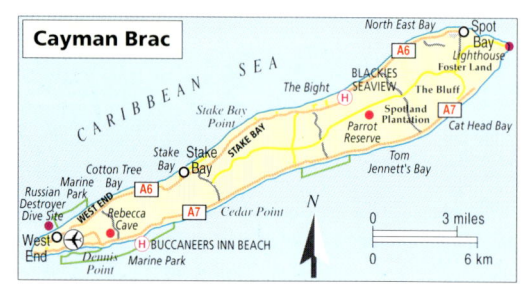

The Bluff ★★

There are fantastic views from this jungle-covered, 140ft (45m) cliff at the island's north end, which is crowned by a small lighthouse. A continuous line of limestone cliffs sweeps away in either direction.

LITTLE CAYMAN

Little Cayman is the next best thing to a private island. About 5 miles (8km) west of Cayman Brac, part of the island's interior is a nature reserve, protecting a host of rare birds – including red-footed boobys, frigate birds, and West Indian whistling ducks – and reptiles such as the wild iguana, as well as plants, including orchids.

Bloody Bay Marine Park ★★★

The park boasts some amazing dive sites ranging from shallow dives on a fantastic coral reef to deep dives on one of the world's finest vertical walls. There are 22 dives in all, with **Great Wall West** rated as the one not to miss. Fish include eagle ray, various groupers, garden eels, plus turtles, brightly coloured sponges, and corals in excellent condition. The marine park is 25 minutes from the handful of resorts on Little Cayman.

Booby Reserve and National Trust House ★★

Flocks of gannet-like boobies and their aerial adversaries, frigate birds, both nest around the shores of this inland mangrove lagoon and can be viewed from the verandah of the pretty wooden National Trust House, which houses a small exhibition on Cayman Brac's environment. Open 09:00–12:00, 15:00–16:30 weekdays.

Tarpon Lake ★★

The giant tarpon, up to 6ft (2m) long and armoured in silver scales up to 1½ inches (3cm) in diameter, is one of the most prized game fishes in the Caribbean. Tarpon are usually marine fish, but a breeding population were trapped in this brackish lagoon, 7½ miles (12km) west of the airstrip, centuries ago when it was cut off from the sea. A wooden walkway leads from the roadside out into the waters of the lagoon.

SILVER THATCH

The **silver thatch palm** is found only on the three Cayman Islands and played an important part in their economy. Until the early 1960s, it was virtually their only cash export. The fibres from the 'tops' – the newest fronds – were dried and twisted into strong, waterproof rope which was exported to Cuba and Jamaica. The tough fronds can also be used for the thatching of houses and weaving hats and baskets. The biggest remaining thatch palm forests are atop the **Bluff**, the highest point of **Cayman Brac**.

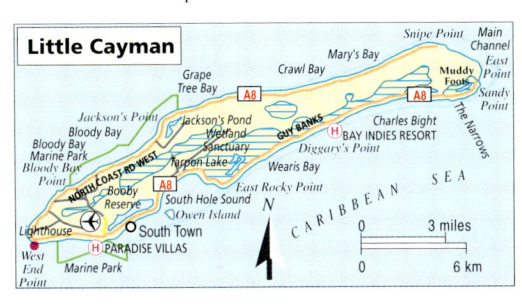

The Cayman Islands at a Glance

BEST TIMES TO VISIT

Visit year-round, but remember that July to September is very hot and damp.

GETTING THERE

Air Jamaica and **Cayman Airways** offer flights between Grand Cayman and Kingston (1hr). Cayman Airways' jets connect Grand Cayman with Miami (90 mins) and Cayman Brac (17 mins). **Island Air** flies Twin Otters between Grand Cayman, Cayman Brac and Little Cayman (45 mins).

GETTING AROUND

By road: Rental companies include Avis, Grand Cayman, tel: 949 2468, fax: 949 7127; Budget, Grand Cayman, tel: 949 5605, fax: 949 2224; Dollar, Grand Cayman, tel: 949 4790, fax: 949 8484; Brac Hertz, Stake Bay, Cayman Brac, tel: 948 1515, fax: 948 1380; McLaughlin Rentals, Little Cayman, tel: 948 1000, fax: 948 1001. **Motorcycles** and **bicycles** may be rented. **Taxis** available, but almost no **buses**. **By sea**: Ferries – Hyatt Dock to Rum Point and Cayman Kai.

WHERE TO STAY

George Town
LUXURY
Best Western/Sammy's Airport Inn, Owen Roberts Drive, PO Box 30746, Seven Mile Beach, tel: 945 2100. Despite the name, an international-standard airport hotel on the outskirts of town. **Coconut Harbour**, PO Box 2086, George Town, tel: 949 7468. Comfortable, waterfront hotel; diving on Waldo's Reef.

MID-RANGE
Ambassadors Inn, PO Box 1789, George Town, tel: 949 7577, fax: 949 7050. Small, central, air-con rooms, pool, dive shop, and dive trips. **Sunset House**, PO Box 479, George Town, tel: 949 7111, fax: 949 7101. Run by divers for divers; outskirts of town.

BUDGET
Enterprise Bed & Breakfast, PO Box 246, Selkirk Drive, Red Bay, Grand Cayman, tel: 947 6009, fax: 947 6010. Affordable, some distance from town centre, but near airport. **Erma Eldemire's Guest House**, PO Box 482, South Church Street, George Town, tel: 949 5569, fax: 949 6987. Family-run; short walk from George Town and beach.

Seven Mile Beach
LUXURY
Caribbean Club, PO Box 11, Seven Mile Beach, tel: 945 4099, fax: 945 4443. Central, no children under 11 in winter. **Hyatt Regency Grand Cayman**, PO Box 1588, Seven Mile Beach, tel: 949 1234, fax: 949 8528. Superb golf course. **Westin Casuarina Resort**, PO Box 30620, tel: 945 3800, fax: 949 5825. Luxury resort on the best stretch of Seven Mile Beach.

MID-RANGE
Beach Club Colony, PO Box 903, George Town, tel: 949 8100, fax: 945 5167. Excellent watersports access. **Windjammer Hotel**, PO Box 30094, Seven Mile Beach, tel: 945 4324, fax: 945 4391. Relaxed and affordable.

BUDGET
White Haven Inn Guest House, PO Box 30424, Seven Mile Beach, tel: 949 1064, fax: 945 4980. Family-owned; away from beach; full US breakfast. **Victoria House**, PO Box 30571, Seven Mile Beach, tel: 945 4233, fax: 945 5328. Affordable condos with up to six beds.

Cayman Brac
LUXURY
Divi Tiara Beach Resort, PO Box 238, Stake Bay, Cayman Brac, tel: 948 1553, fax: 948 1316. Cayman Brac's best, 60 air-con rooms, watersports.

MID-RANGE
La Esperanza, PO Box 28, Stake Bay, Cayman Brac, tel: 948 0531, fax: 948 0525. Five comfortable condominiums.

BUDGET
Walton's Mango Manor, Stake Bay, Cayman Brac, tel/fax: 948 0518. Upmarket; five air-con rooms.

The Cayman Islands at a Glance

Little Cayman
LUXURY
Conch Club Town Homes, PO Box 51, Blossom Village, Little Cayman, tel: 323 8727, fax: 323 8827. Condominiums.
Pirates Point Resort, Preston Bay, Little Cayman, tel: 948 1010, fax: 948 1011. 10-room all-inclusive; diving, dive shop.

MID-RANGE
Paradise Villas, PO Box 30, tel: 948 0001, fax: 948 0002. 12 air-con, one-bedroom condos.

BUDGET
The Cottage, PO Box 35, Blossom Village, tel/fax: 948 0095. Intimate, good value.

WHERE TO EAT

Traditional Caymanian cooking is similar to Jamaican, with fresh seafood, patties, breadfruit, pepperpot, salt fish, ackee and rice and peas on the menu. Conch, a spiral-shelled sea-snail found in local waters, turns up often in fritters, marinated and in chowder.
Diners should note that restaurants rarely have street numbers or addresses, so first call for directions and reservations. Also, on Cayman Brac and Little Cayman, only the hotels have restaurants (*see* Where to Stay).

George Town
LUXURY
The Gourmet, North Church Street, tel: 945 1470. Belgian, French, international cuisine.

Smuggler's Cove, Waterfront, tel: 949 6003. Island dining.
The Crow's Nest, South Sound, tel: 949 9366. Famous for seafood, steaks and curries.

MID-RANGE
Café Tortuga, Galleria Plaza, West Bay Road, tel: 9949 7427. Traditional Caribbean dishes.
Benjamin's Roof, Coconut Place, West Bay Road, tel: 945 4080. Excellent seafood.
Whitehall Bay, Waterfront, tel: 949 8670. Good value.

BUDGET
Subway, Anderson Square, tel: 945 3568. Famed for its island submarine sandwiches.

Seven Mile Beach/West Bay
LUXURY
The Peninsula, Radisson Hotel (*see* Where to Stay), tel: 949 0088. Ocean-front dining.

MID-RANGE
Lantana's, Caribbean Club, West Bay Road, tel: 945 5595. Latin American and Caribbean.

BUDGET
The Coffee Grinder, Seven Mile Shops, tel: 949 4833. Café and bakery.

Fast-food outlets on Seven Mile Beach: **Wendy's**, **Domino's Pizza**, and **Burger King**.

SHOPPING

Duty Free Centre Building, Edward Street, George Town, luxury goods. Do not buy coral or marine jewellery (banned UK, US and other countries).

TOURS AND EXCURSIONS

Rudy's Travellers Transport, PO Box 310, West Bay, Grand Cayman, tel: 949 3208, fax: 949 1155.
Vernon's Sightseeing Tours, PO Box 312, West Bay, Grand Cayman, tel: 949 1509, fax: 949 0213.
Seaborne Flightseeing Adventures, PO Box 2433, Grand Cayman, tel: 949 6029, fax: 949 7044.

USEFUL CONTACTS

Cayman Islands Department of Tourism, The Pavilion, Cricket Square, PO Box 67, George Town, Grand Cayman, tel: 949 0623, fax: 949 4053.

TELEPHONING

International code: **00 345**. All numbers share first digits (**94**), which are omitted for local calls.

CAYMAN ISLES	J	F	M	A	M	J	J	A	S	O	N	D
AVERAGE TEMP. °C	29	29	29	31	31	32	32	32	32	30	27	29
AVERAGE TEMP. °F	84	84	84	88	88	90	90	90	90	86	81	84
HOURS OF SUN DAILY	8	8	8	8	8	7	7	7	6	7	9	9
RAINFALL mm	25	25	25	75	100	75	100	150	150	200	50	25
RAINFALL ins.	1	1	1	3	4	3	4	6	6	8	2	1
DAYS OF RAINFALL	1	1	1	3	4	3	4	6	6	6	2	1

Travel Tips

Tourist Information
JAMAICA
Jamaica Tourist Board offices:
UK: 1–2 Prince Consort Rd, London SW7 2BZ, tel: (0171) 224 0505, fax: (0171) 224 0551.
USA: 1500 N Michigan Ave no. 1030, Chicago, IL 60611, tel: (312) 527 1296, fax: (312) 627 1472; 320 S Dixie Hwy no. 1100, Coral Gables, Miami, FL 33146, tel: (305) 666 0557, fax: (305) 666 7239; 301 2nd Avenue, New York, NY 10017, tel: (212) 866 9727 or (800) 233 4582, fax: (212) 866 9730; 3440 Wilshire Blvd no. 1207, LA, CA 90010, tel: (213) 384 1123, fax: (213) 384 1780.
Canada: 1 Eglinton Ave E no. 616, Toronto, tel: (416) 482 7850, fax: (416) 482 1730.
Head Office: 2 St Lucia Ave, PO Box 360, Kingston 5, Jamaica, tel: (809) 929 9200, fax: (809) 929 9375.

CAYMAN ISLANDS
Cayman Islands Department of Tourism (CIDoT): London, LA, Chicago, Houston, Miami, NY and Toronto.
Head Office: CIDoT, The Pavilion, Cricket Square, PO Box 67, George Town, Grand Cayman, tel: (345) 949 0623, fax: (345) 949 4053.

Entry Requirements
JAMAICA and CAYMAN
No visa required for British, US, Australian, Canadian, and other British Commonwealth or European Union citizens. South African nationals require visas.

Customs
JAMAICA
Duty-free import allowances: 25 cigars, 200 cigarettes, 1 pint (550ml) of liquor, 1 pound of tobacco and 1 quart (1 litre) of wine. Importing rum, coffee and marijuana is forbidden.

CAYMAN ISLANDS
Duty-free import allowances: 1 quart (1 litre) of spirits, 2 bottles of wine, up to 200 cigarettes or equivalent in cigars or tobacco.

Health Requirements
JAMAICA
No special vaccination requirements, but you may want to consider immunization against tetanus, diphtheria, typhoid and hepatitis. Dengue fever (carried by mosquitoes) is present in some locations off the beaten track – no prophylaxis is available for dengue so avoid being bitten.

CAYMAN ISLANDS
No special health precautions.

Getting There
By Air JAMAICA: Air Jamaica flies from London, Miami, and other US airports to Kingston and Mo Bay. British Airways flies between London and Kingston and Mo Bay, and there are many charter flights. American Airlines and United Airlines fly from the US and Canada.

By Air CAYMAN ISLANDS: Air Jamaica and Cayman Airways fly between Kingston and Grand Cayman. Cayman Airways and numerous other US carriers fly between Grand Cayman and Miami and major US and Canadian airports

By Sea: Cruise ships from Miami call at Mo Bay, Kingston, Ocho Rios and Port Antonio in **Jamaica** and at George Town in **Cayman**. There are no regular inter-island **ferries**.

What to Pack
JAMAICA
Beachwear, long-sleeved shirts, a hat, sunscreen and mosquito repellant are essential (all are expensive in Jamaica). Evening-wear ranges from casual (shorts and T-shirt and shorts) to jacket and tie at posh restaurants.

CAYMAN ISLANDS
See Jamaica *above*. You can rent snorkelling and scuba equipment on all three islands.

Money Matters
JAMAICA
Currency: Jamaican dollar notes in denominations of J$1, J$2, J$10, J$20, J$50, J$100, and coins for J$5, J$1, and 50, 25, 20 and 10 cents. Most services are in US dollars, which are widely accepted. US-dollar travellers cheques are preferable to other currencies. Credit cards are widely accepted.
Exchange: Money can be exchanged at banks in major towns, most hotels and the licensed exchange bureaux.

CAYMAN ISLANDS
Currency: Cayman dollar. Most accommodation is priced in US dollars, which are acceptable everywhere as an alternative to local currency. Changing sterling or US dollars into local currency is usually not much of a problem, and major credit cards are accepted by almost all hotels, restaurants, car and bike rental agencies, tour and scuba companies.
Tipping: A 10% tip is normal in most hotels or restaurants. However, some restaurants add a service charge to the bill, in which case there is no need to tip any further. A few all-inclusive resorts follow a no-tipping policy.

Accommodation
JAMAICA
Jamaica has accommodation to suit all holiday budgets, ranging from luxury villas with your own household staff to cheap and cheerful guesthouses and self-catering bungalows and apartments. The most luxurious villas are concentrated around **Port Antonio**, and close to the Hanover coast, west of Montego Bay. **Montego Bay** and **Ocho Rios** have an excellent choice of guesthouse accommodation and mid-to-budget range hotels. **Negril** has by far the biggest choice of simple budget guesthouses and apartments, and even cheaper accommodation can be found around Bluefields and Treasure Beach, on the Westmoreland and St Elizabeth coasts. **Kingston** has a somewhat narrower choice of accommodation for visitors, most of it in the mid-range to upper price brackets and designed mainly with the business traveller in mind. Jamaica pioneered the concept of the **all-inclusive resort,** which has now caught on throughout the Caribbean. At luxury resorts such as those in the Sandals, Couples, and Grand Lido groups and at a number of independently owned imitators, everything from accommodation to unlimited food, drink, land and watersports is included in one fixed package price. There are varying degrees of luxury (for example, some resorts offer only Jamaican alcoholic beverages, while others include imported wines, beers and spirits) and the all-inclusives can offer excellent value for your money. Some of these unique resorts are reserved exclusively for couples, while others cater to families and some are rather notorious for fun-loving singles. These all-inclusive resorts can be found around Montego Bay, Ocho Rios and Negril.

Island Resorts, owned by the Jamaican music industry entrepreneur Chris Blackwell, has some superbly characterful hotels in out of the way places, such as Strawberry Hill in the Blue Mountains and Jake's at Treasure Beach. Jamaica also offers around 40

EMBASSIES AND CONSULATES

JAMAICA
British High Commission
26 Trafalgar Road
Kingston 10
tel (809) 926 9050
Canadian High Commission
30 Knutsford Boulevard
Kingston 5
tel (809) 926 1500
German Embassy
6 St Lucia Avenue
Kingston 5
tel (809) 926 6728
United States Embassy
2 Oxford Road
Kingston 5
tel (809) 926 4850

small **inn-style hotels**, many of them in idyllic locations away from the razzmatazz of the big resorts, grouped under the title 'Inns of Jamaica'. For information on these and all other types of accommodation, contact the Jamaica Tourist Board.

CAYMAN ISLANDS

Grand Cayman has more than 60 places to stay, almost all of them along **Seven Mile Beach**, with a handful elsewhere. Accommodation ranges from budget guesthouses for scuba divers to luxury hotels for the well-heeled traveller, but the accent is definitely on the more **expensive** end of the price scale. Self-catering condominium apartments are substantially cheaper than luxury hotels, and offer a value-for-money compromise, especially for families, with luxury accommodation, landscaped grounds and swimming pools, and fully-equipped kitchens which mean you can save money on food and drink.

Eating Out
JAMAICA

Whether you savour grilled lobster, prawns or red snapper on the beach at Negril, barbecued pork or chicken at a downtown Kingston jerk centre, mouth-watering mangoes with a dash of lime or pineapple dusted with cayenne pepper, Jamaica is at its best when offering deliciously fresh, simply prepared local produce. The island is almost equally good at franchised international fast food, and you'll find no shortage of burgers, pizzas, pasta or fried chicken. Most mid-range hotels and all-inclusive resorts offer buffet meals, with a choice of international and local cuisine such as rice and peas or ackee and saltfish. Kingston has its share of sophisticated restaurants, some of them fostering a new Jamaican style of cooking that makes the most of home-grown produce. Elsewhere, many restaurants tend to place too much emphasis on stylish trappings and not enough on the food, which can be bland and overpriced. All wine is imported, and indifferent wines may be wildly overpriced in more pretentious restaurants.

CAYMAN ISLANDS

Fresh fish and seafood are top of the menu, but Cayman offers everything from local dishes to French, British, Italian, Chinese, American and Mexican cuisine, with most of the restaurants on Grand Cayman close to Seven Mile Beach. Local specialities include the conch, an enormous shellfish – which appears in stews, fritters, marinades and chowder – and breadfruit, which is served boiled, fried, roasted or baked. On Cayman Brac and Little Cayman, almost all restaurants are attached to hotels and guesthouses, and the menu tends to be simpler and a little more limited, but no less well prepared.

Transport
JAMAICA

Air: Air Jamaica's internal services connect Kingston with Montego Bay and Negril (**Air Jamaica**, tel: (809) 923 8680/924 8850). Most domestic flights to and from Kingston operate via Tinson Pen Airport, 2 miles (3km) west of downtown, rather than the international Norman Manley Airport. **Air taxis** can also be chartered to fly you from Montego Bay or Kingston to Negril and smaller airports at Boscobel and Port Antonio.

CONVERSION CHART		
FROM	**TO**	**MULTIPLY BY**
Millimetres	Inches	0.0394
Metres	Yards	1.0936
Metres	Feet	3.281
Kilometres	Miles	0.6214
Kilometres square	Square miles	0.386
Hectares	Acres	2.471
Litres	Pints	1.760
Kilograms	Pounds	2.205
Tonnes	Tons	0.984
To convert Celsius to Fahrenheit: x 9 ÷ 5 + 32		

Road: To rent a car, you will need a valid drivers licence from your country of residence. Roads are generally poor and accidents not uncommon, so you should have comprehensive insurance cover. Drivers must be at least 25 years old and must post a bond (using cash, credit card, or travellers' cheques) to meet insurance requirements. Service stations are open daily and will only accept cash. Speed limit is 30mph (48kph) in built-up areas, 50mph (80kph) on highways. Drive on the left. Road maps area available from the JTB and from the **Jamaican Union of Travellers Association**, 8 Claude Clarke Avenue, PO Box 1155, Montego Bay 1, tel: (809) 968 7088, fax: (809) 974 9142. Driving at night is not recommended.
Bus: Public transport is inadequate, with chaotic schedules, hopelessly overcrowded and poorly maintained vehicles and a good chance of losing at least some of your possessions. Forget it.
Train: The public transport service on the rather rickety railway line which runs between Kingston and Montego Bay – a spectacular ride – has unfortunately been suspended.

CAYMAN ISLANDS
Air: Cayman Airways connects Grand Cayman with Cayman Brac and Little Cayman, as does **Island Air**.

Road: Driving is on the left. Full driving licence and insurance required for rentals. Observe signs for one-way streets in George Town and do not pass stationary buses, as the doors open into the middle of the road (the buses are imported from the US and are designed for driving on the right). Full insurance and collision damage waiver is recommended. Maps are available from the **Cayman Islands Department of Tourism**. There is no motorists' association.

Business Hours
JAMAICA
Banks open 09:00–14:00 Mon–Thur, 09:00–15:00 Fri, with some also open Friday afternoon 14:30–17:00.
Offices usually open 09:00–17:00 Mon–Fri and **shops** open 08:30–17:00 Mon–Sat, with a half-day on Wednesday.

CAYMAN ISLANDS
Banks open 09:00–13:00, 14:00–16:00 Mon–Fri.
Government offices open 09:00–17:00 Mon–Fri.
Shops mostly open 08:30–12:00 and 14:00–17:00, half day Saturday, closed Sunday, but many of the duty-free shops may have longer shopping hours.

Time Difference
Both **Jamaica** and the **Cayman Islands** are on US Eastern Standard Time: GMT –6 (spring/summer), GMT –5 (autumn/winter).

> **ROAD SIGNS**
>
> Road signs in **Jamaica** are few and far between and navigation can be a challenge. **Cayman** uses a mixture of British and US-style signage, employing words as well as symbols.

Communications
JAMAICA
The external dialling code for all Jamaican telephone numbers is **809**. All the upmarket hotels have direct dial. Telephone service in theory operates 24hr a day but the system is overstretched and it can be difficult to get a connection at peak times. Operator assistance: tel: **112** (local) or **113** (international). There are no 24hr post offices in Jamaica. Fax facilities are available in almost all the hotels and guesthouses.

CAYMAN ISLANDS
For international calls to the Cayman Islands dial the code **00 345**). All Grand Cayman, Cayman Brac and Little Cayman telephone and fax numbers share the same first two digits (**94**), which are omitted for local calls. Telephone service operates 24hr a day. No 24hr post offices. Fax facilities available from all major hotels.

Electricity
Jamaica and the **Caymans** use US current and electrical fittings, 110/115 volt, 60-cycle current.

Holidays and Festivals

JAMAICA
New Year's Day • Ash Wednesday • Good Friday • Easter Monday • Labour Day (23 May) • Independence Day (first Monday in Aug) • National Heroes' Day (third Mon in Oct) • Christmas Day • Boxing Day.
Festivals:
Reggae SunSplash (usually in Aug)

CAYMAN ISLANDS
New Year's Day • Ash Wednesday • Good Friday • Easter Monday • Discovery Day (19 May) • the Queen's Birthday • Constitution Day (7 July) • Remembrance Day (November) • Christmas Day and Boxing Day.
Festivals:
Easter Regatta • Million Dollar Month Fishing Tournament (June) • Cayman Islands International Aviation Week (June/July) • Pirates Week Festival (October)

Weights and Measures
Jamaica and the **Cayman Islands** officially use old-fashioned British Imperial weights and measures (pounds and ounces for weight, pints and gallons for liquids) but as almost everything is imported from the US, most quantities are in US pounds, ounces and fluid measures (fluid ounces, pints, quarts and gallons). Distances are non-metric.

Health Precautions
No special health precautions are required by law for either of the destination. Tap water is safe to drink in both **Jamaica** and the **Cayman Islands**. Visitors from cooler climes should beware sunburn and heat exhaustion (especially in the Caymans, where shade can be in short supply); use adequate sunscreen and drink plenty of fluids.
To be safe, some visitors may choose to have themselves and their family vaccinated against tetanus, diphtheria, typhoid and hepatitis, although these precautions are seldom essential. *See also* Health Requirements *on p. 122*.

Health Services
Good, modern health services in clinics and hospitals are available in both **Jamaica** and the **Cayman Islands**, but adequate medical insurance cover is essential as medical services are extremely costly.

Security
JAMAICA
Jamaica has an extremely high rate of violent crime (more than 900 murders a year) and tourists, especially those who dabble in drug purchases, are far from immune. Walking any distance after dark is not advised, and ghetto areas of urban Kingston should be avoided at all times. Incidents may be reported to local police stations.

CAYMAN ISLANDS
Cayman is one of the safest places in the world, with very little violent crime and only a small amount of petty pilfering. Valuables should be kept in hotel safes or safe deposits.

Emergencies
JAMAICA
Police: dial **911**
Fire and ambulance: dial **110**

CAYMAN ISLANDS
All emergencies: dial **911**

Language
English is the official language of Jamaica and the Cayman Islands, although Jamaicans Frequently speak in patois to each other, which is virtually incomprehensible to foreigners.

Good Reading

Leonard Barrett
Rastafarians: The Dreadlocks of Jamaica (Heinemann, 1977).
Frank Bernal *Birds of Jamaica* (Heinemann Caribbean, 1989). Definitive guide to Jamaican birdlife
Hugh O'Shaughnessy *Around the Spanish Main*, (Century, 1991). Travels in the Caribbean.
Malika Whitney and Dermott Hussey *Bob Marley: Reggae King of the World* (Kingston Publishers, 1984).
Lawson Wood *Dive Sites of the Cayman Islands* (New Holland, 1995).

INDEX

Note: Numbers in **bold** indicate photographs

accommodation 46, 60–61, 74, 78, 88–89, 96, 100–101, 111, 120–121, 123
ackee 29, 53
African Caribbean Institute (see Institute of Jamaica)
agriculture 5, 16, 20, 67, 97, 103, 107
Alligator Pond 97, 107
American Civil War 16
Anansi 85
Antilles, Lesser 12
Appleton Estate 91, 98
Arawak 6, 10, 11, 14, 66, 99, 103, 108, **110**
architecture 36, 40, 41, 67, 69, 82, 83, 105, 109
art 24–29, 33, 34, 37, 67, 78, 105
Athenry Gardens 52

Banton, Buju 26
Barbados 14
Barnett Estate 77, 80
Bath 56
beaches 50, 55, 63, **64**, 65, 71, 73, 77, 78, 79, 80, 81, 91, 92, 94, 103, 107, 110, 113, 117, **118**, 124
Belvedere Estate 82
birds 9, 43, 59, 65, 81, 83, 84, 95, 98, 116, 119
Bishop's Lodge 37
Black River 91, **97**, 98, 99
Black Star Line 15
Bloody Bay 92
Bluefields 91, 96
Blue Hole 49, **52**
Blue Mountains–John Crow Mountains National Park 32, 44
Bogle, Paul 10, 17, 57, 79
  Monument 58, **59**
Booby Cay 95
botanical gardens
  Bath 56
  Castleton 42, **43**
  Cinchona 43
  Hope 35, 38
buccaneers 13, 14, 39 (see also piracy)

Bustamante, Alexander 10, 17, 18, 59

Cardiff Hall 71
Carib 9, 10, 11, 12
Carlisle Bay 10
Cathedral of St Jago 103
Caymanas Park 110
Cayman Islands 6, 22, 28, 112–121
  Bloody Bay Marine Park 114, 119
  Bluff, The 118, 119
  Booby Reserve 119
  Cayman Brac 114, 117, 119
  George Town 114, 116, 117
  Grand Cayman 113, 116, 117
  Little Cayman 114, 119
  Mastic Trail 113, 116
  National Trust House 119
  North West Point 116
  Queen Elizabeth II Botanic Park 116
  Seven Mile Beach 113, 114, 115, 116, **117**
  Stake Bay 117
  Stingray City **112**, 113, 116
  Tarpon Lake 119
  Turtle Farm 113, 116, 117
Christiana 106
Chukka Cove 71
Clarendon Parish 103–110
Cliff, Jimmy 25, 26, 27
climate 6, 8–9, 21, 32, 46, 60, 74, 88, 100, 104, 105, 111, 113, 120, 121
coasts 49, 50, 52, 57, 63, 83, 110, 113
Cockpit Country 5, 7, 49, 77, 84–85, 91, 98, 99
coffee 21, **44**, 105
Colbeck Castle **108**
Columbus, Christopher 11, **12**, 53, 70, 73, 108, 113
Comfort Castle 54
consulates 123
Cornwall 77, 91
Cornwall Beach 80
Coromantee 10, 15, 54
Coward, Sir Noel 63, 67, 69
crafts 35, 41, 109
crocodiles 9, 83, **84**, 97
crops 20, 21, 67
cruises 8, **19**, 65, 81, 122

Cudjoe 10, 15, 17, 98
cuisine 29, 46–47, 53, 61, 75, 88–89, 94, 100–101, 105, 111, 121, 124
Cultural Training Centre 34
culture 24–29, 67, 78, 118, 122

Daniels River 53
Devon House 31, **36**
Discovery Bay 63, 73
diving 28, 101, 113, 114, **116**
Doctor's Cave Beach 79, **80**
dreadlocks 23, 25
Dunn's River Falls 55, 63, **66**, 75
duppies 99

earthquake 14, 38, 39, 40
economy 10, 16, 17, 19–21, 104, 105, 113, 115, 123
embassies 123
emigration 20

Falmouth 83–84
Farquhar's Beach 107
Fern Gully 66
ferries 39, 51, 53, 122
festivals 126
film 27, 68
Firefly 63, 69
Fish River 95
Fishermen's Beach 39
fishing 39, 50, 51, 55, 66, 93, **97**, 107, 110
flag 59
Flint River 86
Flynn, Errol 27, 50, 51, 53
food (see cuisine)
Fort Charles **41**
Fort Charlotte 87
Fort Clarence Beach 110
Fort George 50
Freeport Peninsula 81
Friends of the Sea 71
fruit 42, 56

ganja (see marijuana)
Garvey, Marcus Mosiah **15**, **70**
Ginger Town 54
God's Well 52
golf 28, 71, 77, 86, 113, 115, 116
Good Hope Plantation 84
Gordon Town 45

government 6, 19–21, 103, 109, 115
Great Morass (Black River) 9, 91, 97
Great Morass (Negril) 95
Great River **6**, **76**, 77, 80, 86
Green Grotto 63, 72
Greenwood Great House 82, **83**

Hanover Parish 7, 77–89
Harmony Hall 63, **67**
Hellshire 110
higglers 34, 55, 72
hiking 32, 33, 110, 114, 115
Hollywell Forest Park 43
hot springs 56, 107
hotels 46, 60–61, **65**, 68, 74–75, 78, 88–89, 94, 96, 106, 111, 120–121
hurricanes 9
  Gilbert 9, 10, 43

Industrial Trade Union 17
Institute of Jamaica 33, 34
Island Outpost 69

Jamaica Defence Force 43
Jamaica House 36–37
Jamaica Safari Village 83, **84**
Jamaica Tourist Board 21, 37, 47, 54, 61, 70, 75, 80, 89, 95, 101, 111
Jamaican Labour Party (JLP) 10, 17, 18, 19
Jamaican National Heritage Trust 59, 69

King's House 36–37, 108
Kingston 5, 7, 10, 13, 18, 20, 23, 24, 26, 30–38, 46–47

language 22, 23, 25, 126
Long Bay 52, **55**, 92, 94, 95, 107
Lovers' Leap 99
Lucea 85, 87
Lyssons Beach 57

MacIntosh, Peter 'Tosh' 26
Mallard's Bay 65
Manchester Parish 103–110
Manchioneal 55
Mandeville 20, 103, 104–106

INDEX

Marshall's Pen Great House 103, **106**
marijuana **21**, 23, 33, 44, 97, 104
markets 31, 34, **35**, 79, 89, 94
Marley, Bob 19, 24, 25, 26, **27**, 34, 35, 72, 80, 99
Museum 31, **37**
Maroon 5, 10, 13, 15, 25, 49, 54, 59, 84, 85, 91, 98, 99
Martha Brae River 84, **85**
May Pen 107–108
Milk River 107
mining **20**, 104
Mo Bay (see Montego Bay)
Montego Bay 5, 8, 16, 20, 64, 75, 77, 78–80, **81**
Montego River 78, **81**
Moore Town 54
Morant Bay **17**, 57, **58**
Morgan's Harbour Hotel **42**
mountains 7, 44, 45, 49, 54, 86, 99, 104
museums 31, 33, 37, 40, 54, 66, 72, 97, 103, 109
music 24–26, 32

Naggo Heads 110
Nanny 17, 54
Nanny Town 54
National Gallery 24, **33**
Navy Island **51**, 53, 60
Negril 5, 8, 16, **91**, 92–95, 99
New Kingston 35–38
New Seville (see Sevilla la Nueva)
Newcastle Fort 43
Nine Mile 72

Obeah 23

Ocho Rios 8, **19**, 27, 55, 63, 64–68, 104
Old Assembly House 108
Orange River 95
Oracabessa 68, 75

Palisadoes Peninsula 38, 42
parliament 35
Parottee Point 99
People's National Party (see PNP)
piracy 14, 39, 41, 93, 95
plantations 5, 67, 68, 71, 82, 84, 86, 97, 98
plants 42, 43, 56, **57**, 65, 86, 87, 106, 116, 119
PNP 10, 17, 18, 19
Port Antonio 5, 8, 19, **49**, 50–52, 55, 64
Port Maria 68–69
Port Morant 57
Port Royal 10, 14, 31, 32, 38–42, 46–47
Portland Parish 49–61
Portmore 110
Prospect Plantation 67
Puerto Seco Beach 73

Rackham, John 'Calico Jack' 41, 93, 95
rafting 52, **53**, 61, **76**, 77, 84, 89
Rastafarianism 22, 33, 38, 44, 72, 107
rebellion 10, 15, 17, 57, 69, 79, 98
reggae 23, 25, 26, 27, 79, 81, 94
religion **22**, 23, 67, 107
Rio Bueno 63
Rio Grande 5, 7, 49, 51, 53
road signs 125
Rose Hall Great House 81, 82

Roselle Beach 57
rum 29, 45, 98
Runaway Bay 63, 71–72
Rutland Point 95

Sabina Park 28
San San Beach 52
Sandy Bay 85
Sandy Beach Bay 66
Santa Cruz Mountains 99
Santiago de la Vega (see Spanish Town)
Savanna-La-Mar 95
Seaford Town 96
Seaman's Valley 54
Seawind Beach Resort 81
Sevilla la Nueva 10, 63, 71, 108
Sharpe, Sam 'Daddy' 10, **16**, 17, 54, 79
Shaw Park 65
Shooter's Hill 105
shopping 47, 61, 75, 78, 81, 89, 101, 121
Somerset Falls 55
South Negril Point 92, 95
Spanish Town 13, 20, 31, 103, 108–110
sport 27–28, 71, 97, 101, 110, 113, 116
St Andrew Parish 30–31, 42–43, 46–47
St Ann Parish 11, 63–75
St Elizabeth Parish 9, 91, 97–101
St James Parish 7, 77–89
St Margaret's Bay 53
St Mary Parish 63–75
St Thomas Parish 49–61
sugar 10, **14**, 16, 20, 63, 67, 84, 86, 98, 108
Sulphur River 56

Tacky 15, 69

Teach, Edward 'Blackbeard' 39, 41
theatre 32, 35, 69
Titchfield Peninsula 51
Tivoli Gardens 33
transport 46, 60, 74, 88, 100, 111, 120, 122, 124–125
travel companies 47, 61, 75, 89, 101
Treasure Beach 91, 99
Treaty of Madrid 13, 114
Trelawny Parish 77–89
Trench Town 26, 33
Tryall 28
Golf Club 77, **86**
Water Wheel 86
Turtle Beach 65

unemployment 20, 33

Villa de la Vega 63, 108, 109

Wailers, The 25, 26, 27
Walter Fletcher Beach 79
Ward Theatre 35
waterfalls 53, 55, 64, 66, 97
watersports 42, 66, 101, 113
West Harbour 51
West End 92, **93**
Westmoreland Parish 91–97
wetlands 95, 96, 97, 110
White River 63
wildlife 9, 87, 93, 97, 110, 117, 119
William Grant Park 35
Wyndham Hotel **35**, 46

yachting 51, 113
YS River **98**
Falls 5, 91, 97